THE MEDITERRANEAN
IN THE
ANCIENT WORLD

AN ALEXANDRIAN GRAIN SHIP
From a Sidonian sarcophagus, probably of the second century A.D.

(From Dr G. Contenau: *La Civilisation phénicienne*, Payot, Paris, Editeur.)

THE MEDITERRANEAN
IN THE
ANCIENT WORLD

BY

J. HOLLAND ROSE, Litt.D.

Vere Harmsworth Professor of Naval History
and Fellow of Christ's College in the University
of Cambridge; Hon. LL.D. of the University of
Manchester, of the University of Nebraska, and
of Amherst College, Mass.

GREENWOOD PRESS, PUBLISHERS
NEW YORK

First published in 1934

Reprinted by permission
of the Cambridge University Press

First Greenwood Reprinting 1969

Library of Congress Catalogue Card Number 69-14061

SBN 8371-1933-2

PRINTED IN UNITED STATES OF AMERICA

CONTENTS

PREFACE

In this book I make no attempt to construct a naval history of the Mediterranean peoples; for the materials are scrappy and often untrustworthy. Besides, we cannot fully appreciate the motives which actuated the ancients in sea affairs. Our confidence, born of age-long experience and advance in craftsmanship, was wanting to them; they looked on even the usually placid summer Mediterranean with the inner dread of children seeking to cajole a monster with toys. Also, naval questions were then often decided by motives which are incomprehensible to us. Religion prompted Agamemnon to sacrifice his daughter in order to ensure the raising of a wind which would bear the Greek armada Troy-wards; and, 600 years later, an eclipse of the moon induced the highly cultured Athenians to let slip the last opportunity of escaping from the death trap at Syracuse. Can we ever fully understand naval policy working in such a limbo?

There were other complicating and little known factors, such as the inadequate man-power of the city States of the Greeks and Phœnicians, also the difficulties of ensuring a steady supply of seasoned timber and metals for construction, of providing food and drink against a long voyage, and of building up a reserve of oarsmen sufficient to make good the wastage of even an ordinary campaign (see Thucydides, VII, 14). Is it surprising that the

Greek city States and even Carthage, which relied on mercenaries, often wavered in face of these costly and man-devouring demands? They knew well enough the potent effects of sea control, witness the statements of Herodotus concerning Minos, Polycrates, the Aeginetans, and the crises in the invasion of Greece by Xerxes. Thucydides, who also hailed in Minos the first of sea powers, rightly discerned in that seaman-statesman, Themistocles, the saviour of Greece from Persia. As his tactics at Salamis conduced to that momentous victory, I have described them fully as illustrating his skill in utilizing the peculiarities of his coast-line against an eastern despot who ignored them. Nevertheless, Athens showed little intelligence or steadiness in her subsequent use of the trident; she threw away two fleets and armies on the mad Syracusan venture, and at Ægospotami was ruined by a fairly obvious trick practised by her less clever enemy. Rhodes is the only Greek State that deserves credit for acting consistently as a sea power; for she not only maintained her fleets steadily and skilfully, but adapted her general policy wisely to naval resources and commercial needs. Of Rhodes, however, we know too little to reconstruct adequately that fragment of Greek life.

The same may be said of the elusive annals of Tyre and Sidon; while their offspring, Carthage, however great in commerce, failed utterly at her first clash with a people quite unused to the sea.

Here again I have sought to expand my narrative; for it concerns the sphere of national character, which is too often left out of count in naval affairs. Indeed, I regard this First Punic War as (next to that of Xerxes) the greatest of the ancient world, both in respect to the war fitness of the two opposing peoples, and to the immeasurable greatness of the results obtained by victorious Rome. On the other hand, I pass over the Peloponnesian War, because, contrary to the initial assertion of Thucydides, I consider that its results were little more than local and temporary, except in so far as it weakened the Greek race.

While I have not sought to write naval history, I have tried to explain the natural advantages favouring early man in his long struggle with the sea; also to point out the salient facts in the development of the ship—from the four days' effort of Odysseus to the great Alexandrian corn ship in which St Paul was wrecked. I have also dwelt on topographical factors, especially the immense importance of the command of the two chief straits, the Hellespont and Messina. In fact, the supremacy of Rome was assured by her firm grip of those key positions, which others had neglected or toyed with loosely. Both in her central position, in her vast reserves of strength and in her ultimately intelligent and persistent use of it, she is the only State of antiquity which deserves to rank as a great and efficient sea power. The others failed in one or more of the factors making for supremacy. Accordingly, I have traced in some detail her maritime progress, which dwarfs that of the city States of Greece and Phœnicia, or that of the Hellenistic monarchies. Yet, after winning political supremacy, even she relaxed her energies until the pirates' grip on her foreign corn supplies compelled her to adopt those persistent efforts at sea which alone can exert lasting influence on civilization. How greatly that influence of Rome rested on sea control has, I believe, never been adequately set forth; and to contrast it with the relatively weak and fitful efforts of earlier peoples is my chief object. I have tried to interest not only classical scholars but also the general reader.

In this difficult inquiry I have received valuable advice and criticism on different parts of the subject from the following Cambridge men: Professor F. E. Adcock of King's College, Professor F. C. Burkitt of Trinity College, Professor A. B. Cook of Queens' College, and Messrs H. H. Brindley and M. P. Charlesworth of St John's College, and E. H. Warmington, now of King's College, London; also from Mr H. T. Wade-Gery, sub-Warden of Wadham College, Oxford, and the Rev. A. M. Perkins. While not accepting all their conclusions, I tender to them heartfelt thanks; but, of course, the responsibility for the narrative rests

on me alone.   My thanks are due also to Dr Georges
Contenau and his publishers, Messrs Payot, for permission to reproduce as frontispiece the Alexandrian
grain ship taken from his work, *La Civilisation
phénicienne*.

J. H. R.

CAMBRIDGE
November 1932

CHAPTER I

THE MEDITERRANEAN AS THE NURSERY FOR NAVIGATION

Man does not by nature take to the sea. He needs to be tempted on to that alien element. And of all the seas the Mediterranean has been the arch-temptress. While the boisterous, tide-swept oceans scared away all but the superman of primitive races, the inland sea sang her siren song with kindly intent and promised him mastery over another world.

We will pass over the remote age when that sea was separated from the Ocean and was divided, near Sicily, into two great lakes; and we will seek to understand its characteristics when it occupied the present basin. It is so shut off from the Ocean that little or no tidal impulse enters. The Mediterranean tide rarely rises more than a foot,[1] except at the head of narrowing gulfs, where, as at Venice, the rise may amount to 2 ft. or more. Therefore the inland sea is almost free from the tidal currents which baffled and terrified the oarsmen of primitive times if they ventured outside its western portals.[2] In that vast lake, enclosed by the shores of the then known world, they found few strong currents, the skies were nearly always clear, and during the

[1] Strabo, I, 3, par. 82.
[2] Vegetius, F. (*De Re militari*, ch. 12), notes that oars cannot surmount the tides.

months of summer light winds or calms prevailed. Nowhere else were waters so safe and climatic conditions so favourable for the vessel propelled by oars; and this was especially the case in the eastern half, with which we are at first more specially concerned; for it has the characteristics of a landlocked sea, while those of the Atlantic often intrude into the weather of the West Mediterranean.

Moreover the northern shores of this inland sea are serrated by three great peninsulas, in two of which are many sheltering gulfs. The north coast of Africa, it is true, presents an almost unbroken front, which, except at two points, has discouraged navigation and hindered the progress of its peoples; but on the European side sea and land intermingle to an extent nowhere else to be found. From the coast of Cilicia to that of Spain there occurs a long succession of capes and bays, islands and islets, which invite, nay almost compel, intercourse by sea.

At the outset I wish to emphasize these dominating facts. For the contrast between the almost harbourless land-mass of Africa and the myriad interlacings of sea and land on the opposite coast goes far to explain the static life of Africa and the progressive civilization of Europe. Progress depends very largely on the free interchange of the inventions and products of diverse peoples and climes; and such interchange can best be effected by sea—a statement which is fundamental to the whole of our present inquiry. I will go further and assert that the history of nations has been far too much written from the standpoint of the land; whereas maritime environment counts for as much as the character of the land.

Spread out a good physical map and consider the great advantages of Southern Europe in this respect. Its peninsulas and islands, diversifying the Mediterranean, have from the earliest age challenged men to voyage from one to the other; and during nearly half the year the challenge was friendly. For that broken coastline presents few dangers, the land being generally mountainous or undulating and sloping down into deep water. Also the headlands have not there been subjected to the tidal scour of ages, which has strewn beneath our ever-wasting capes the reefs so fatal to coastwise traffickers. And under the lee of Mediterranean headlands there is deposited little *detritus*, so that their bays are seldom masked by shoals which form another peril of our home waters. Apart from the silt poured forth by its semi-torrential rivers, the coasts of that sea present very few dangers. Well may that lover of the Mediterranean, Joseph Conrad, write of it as "that tideless basin, freed from hidden shoals and treacherous currents", which has "led mankind gently from headland to headland, from bay to bay, from island to island, out into the promise of world-wide oceans".[1]

[1] Conrad, J., *The Mirror of the Sea*, p. 187.

Even so, primitive man probably did not put out to sea if the land furnished all his needs.[1] As to the motives which led him on to maritime quests we may learn much from primitive tribes surviving in recent times. Some of them were, or are still, in the Stone Age; and, if they have lived in isolation, they live the life of man, say, 10,000 years ago. Generally they are hunters, pursuing their prey with what seem to us poor weapons. And, naturally, if they do succeed, it tends to thin down. What happens then? They take to fishing. Now, there are signs which show that fishing comes later than hunting, at least for several peoples. Thus, there was no word for fish among the original Indo-European peoples. Also the Achæans, who invaded Greece from the North, are represented by Homer as eating fish only in the extremity of hunger.[2] Vast supplies of flesh constituted the ideal Homeric banquet.

Probably the pressure of hunger drove primitive peoples to fish in marshes and rivers; and in course of time they learnt to make canoes of reeds from which they speared fish or drove them into shallows and then netted them. Coast-dwelling tribes found that fish were plentiful in the shallows of the sea;

[1] I question the dictum of Köster, A., in *Das antike Seewesen*, p. 1, that navigation is as old as man himself; for the evidence as to the ways of primitive man seems to show that he was first of all a hunter by land.

[2] *Odyssey*, XII, 331; Rose, H. J., *Primitive Culture in Greece*, p. 141.

they constructed larger canoes, sometimes of bundles of bark, lashed together with long grass or withies. Thus, the French expedition of 1800 to Australia found the very primitive native Tasmanians fishing in canoes of eucalyptus bark, one of which was 15 ft. by 5 ft. and ventured well out to sea, propelled by six men with poles. A raft of bark and reeds, twice as long, would go over rough water to an island three miles out.[1] Examples of similar devices are widespread, and reed rafts or canoes are still in use in marshes, rivers and even off shore in many parts of the world.

As reeds and suitable tree-bark are not common on the coasts of the Mediterranean, reed-rafts and bark-boats were little used in that sea—a fortunate circumstance, seeing that little progress can be made with those materials. But on its shores there is, or rather was, until goat and Turk played havoc with it, fair store of good timber, also of stone capable of taking a good edge and therefore of cutting and working up wood. Consequently, even before the age of metals, Mediterranean man learnt to make wooden canoes, probably first by hollowing out the trunks of trees. These "dug-outs" were far more seaworthy than canoes made of rushes, skins or bark;

[1] See *Atlas* of Péron's, *Voyage...aux Iles Australes*, 1800–4, also *Mariner's Mirror*, xvii, No. 1, for this and other specimens of primitive canoes. Note also that very early Egyptian ships are shown as being bound together with rushes. Reed-rafts and thence canoes were certainly the earliest Nile craft.

and as late as 400 B.C. "dug-outs" (μονόξυλα πλοῖα) were found by Xenophon in use by a tribe on the south-east of the Euxine, which brought 300 such craft to help the Greeks. Seeing that Xenophon describes the tribe as possessing good stores of salted dolphin and dolphin blubber, they clearly used these "dug-outs" for fishing in the Euxine.[1]

Later, we shall see how the Greeks of the Homeric Age fashioned their craft. But during many centuries before the time of Homer, neolithic man made his way about the Mediterranean; for wherever fine flint, obsidian or greenstone can be worked, there primitive man was able to make sharp-edged tools suitable for constructing large canoes and boats, as the great war canoes of the Maori convincingly prove. Flint and obsidian are found on Mediterranean coasts, and by tools made from them early man probably soon built seaworthy craft. Ethnologists even consider that the Mediterranean peoples form a distinct family.[2] It may have spread originally from North Africa to Crete, the Ægean lands and thence westwards; and some archæologists maintain that neolithic man ventured out on the Ocean to Britain and Ireland; but, in the present uncertain

[1] Xenophon, *Anabasis*, v, 4. On the growth of the dug-out canoe see Fawcett, C. B., "The Evolution of Navigation", in *Manch. Geograph. Soc. Journal*, 1921.

[2] *Camb. Ancient Hist.* I, 110; Breasted, J. H., *Ancient Times*, pp. 226–8.

state of our knowledge, I pass over this topic. My present aim is, not ethnological, but maritime, especially to suggest the motives which led Mediterranean man to take to the sea.

The primary impulse for all this effort and adventure was, in all probability, search after food. For, if the people of the Eastern Mediterranean ran short of flesh or corn, they were compelled to resort to the sea; and that often happened, owing to the rocky or sandy nature of many of the coasts, which yield scanty harvests, or in years of drought no harvest at all. Further, the forests of the coastal areas were not so extensive as to support very large supplies of game. Therefore the early tribes which were driven by their enemies to the shores of the Mediterranean must have had a constant struggle for food. Naturally, the conquered tribes had recourse to the sea for food; and it is significant that conquering peoples long retained their contempt for seafarers. In Homer the fisherman had no social status such as the farmer had;[1] and, even among the island Phæacians, the champion wrestler, Euryalus, taunts the castaway Odysseus with being a mere sea-trader, intent only on greedy gains, and no sportsman.[2]

Slowly did the conquering Achæans and Dorians who came from the North learn the difficult art of seafaring from the conquered Ægean folk, who,

[1] Radcliffe, W., *Fishing from the Earliest Times*, pp. 64–8.
[2] *Odyssey*, viii, 163.

along with the Minoans, must have practised it for ages. We know next to nothing about those primitives, who made the first incredibly difficult attempts at rowing and sailing. Minoan signet rings show quaint little boats with high prows and sterns, propelled by oarsmen. It seems likely that the first of these efforts were directed towards fishing; for on the warm coasts of the Mediterranean one of the largest and fattest of fish abounds. The tunny (a huge fish not unlike a giant mackerel) has there been speared and netted during thousands of years. Yet it is still plentiful; and even now the yachtsman is warned to beware of tunny nets spread out from the shore at scores of places in Syria, the Tripolitan, the Ægean, and as far west as Sicily.[1] Spawned mostly in the Sea of Azov or the North Euxine, the fish swim south through the Marmara to the Mediterranean, where they attain a huge size, often turning 400 lb. or more.[2]

Now, consider the food value of a single fat tunny in lands where goat was none too common a dish, and where the ox was generally a skinny little beast. Picture to yourselves the stimulus to the building of larger boats, stronger nets or lines, and bigger hooks or harpoons of which that fish was the reluctant

[1] *Mediterranean Pilot*, i, 27, 321; v, 55.
[2] One of the signs of Poseidon was the tunny (Cook, A. B., *Zeus*, p. 786). In August 1932 Col. E. T. Peel caught off Scarborough a tunny $9\frac{1}{3}$ ft. long, weighing 798 lbs.

cause. The harpooning of the tunny or the chasing of a shoal of tunny into creeks or shallows became a favourite sport of the Greeks; for Aristophanes (*Wasps*, l. 1087) uses the word θυννάζειν as equivalent to harpooning; and Æschylus in the *Persae* (l. 427) drove home to the Athenian audience the slaughter of the beaten Persians at Salamis by comparing them to tunnies driven inshore and speared by fishermen.

But this is not all. The tunny, as we have seen, swam down the Bosporus, Propontis and Hellespont in shoals towards the warm waters of the Ægean and South Mediterranean; and I imagine that no small share of man's early seafaring energies went to the pursuit of those shoals. At the risk of unduly stressing this tunny *motif*, I will suggest another service which this fish has rendered to mankind. Its shoals, as we have seen, come regularly from the Sea of Azov and Euxine down the Bosporus and Hellespont to the Ægean. Is it not certain that fishermen would try to find out where they came from and where they went to? Surely, then, the first seafarers up and down those straits would be tunny fishermen. The first explorers of the Euxine were, I suggest, not Jason and the Argonauts (the men of the golden fleece), but the pioneer tunny-chasers —the men of the bronze harpoon.[1]

[1] See, however, Miss J. R. Bacon's careful monograph, *The Voyage of the Argonauts*.

Perhaps, even earlier, the tunny, which still abounds off the north coast of Africa and now provides one of the chief industries for that barren land,[1] may have tempted on to the sea its primitive inhabitants. As we have seen, these may have spread thence northwards to Asia Minor or Europe. If this view be correct, may not the poverty of North Africa (except in the Nile Delta and Tunis) and the riches of the sea have driven and lured those peoples northwards? Here it is well to remember that, though the Etesian breezes of summer, blowing from the north-north-west, retard the northerly voyage, yet they scarcely affect the Syrian coast, where also a northerly current of from one to two knots favours the coastal run towards Asia Minor, and so enables the trader from the Ægean to make a round trip to Egypt, Syria and thence home again.[2] So soon as man had observed the set of the winds and currents, he had these forces as his allies in the Eastern Mediterranean, probably first for fishing, and later for trading.

That this was the order in which seafaring developed may be inferred from these facts: (1) hunger is the primal cause of man's activities: the search for clothing, ornaments and weapons comes later; (2) though Homer mentions fish as a diet (and in the Ægean area that implies sea fish) yet he rarely, if ever, mentions sea-traders other than Phœnicians

[1] *Mediterranean Pilot*, v, 55.   [2] *Ibid.* v, 135, 156.

and, as we have seen, often with contempt. In his age, apparently, the Greeks had not taken up sea-borne commerce; yet, as will appear later, the presence of amber and bronze in the Minoan and Egyptian palaces proves that their predecessors had for ages traded with the Adriatic and the Western Mediterranean.

To sum up—the Eastern Mediterranean presents four conditions which partly compelled and partly tempted early man to venture on its waters. These conditions were: (1) comparatively barren shores, often liable to droughts and therefore to famines; (2) coastal waters which abound in fish—one being of high food value; (3) absence of tidal currents, also generally calm weather from April to October; (4) Etesian breezes in the height of summer, offset by the northerly current along the Syrian shore—a condition which favoured the triangular voyage from Greece to Crete and Egypt, and back by way of Syria, Cyprus and under the lee of Asia Minor to the shelter of the Sporades; (5) a fair supply of timber for boat-building, but relative scarcity of the precious metals, also of tin and iron—a condition which tempted man to make longer and longer voyages in search of ornaments for his women, tools for farm work and weapons for war.

Let us now try to understand the impulse to trade, and therefore to navigation, which results from these conditions. First, the triangular voyage noted above must have benefited trade greatly; for such a voyage favours the chance of picking up produce of diverse kinds and of profitable freighting throughout the whole venture, which was generally based on the carriage of tin and amber to the Levant.

Signs of the traffic in tin and amber which went on from the head of the Adriatic and then behind its islands and those of the Ionian Sea to Corinth, prove that man very early discovered the safest way of bringing the tin of North-west Spain (perhaps also of Britain) together with the amber of the Baltic to the palaces of Minos and the Pharaohs.[1] The Adriatic is often a gusty and dangerous sea; but its string of islands provides much shelter, which is to be found also down to the entrance of the Gulf of Corinth. Transit over the isthmus, and thence across the Ægean with the favouring Etesian winds, facilitated the trade to Crete and thence to Egypt. Such seems to be the easiest route by which Baltic amber could reach Crete and Egypt. Probably that miracle of transport occurred before 2000 B.C.

Early in his coastings man devised means for evading the swift current of the Hellespont—a topic

[1] Evans, Sir A., *The Palace of Minos*, I, 17; II, 70–90, 166–170, 176–180, 240; Navarro, J., "Prehistoric Routes between N. Europe and Italy, defined by the Amber Trade", in *R. Geograph. Journal*, 1925; also Childe, V. Gordon, *The Bronze Age*, pp. 46–52.

reserved for the next chapter—and for avoiding the terrors of Charybdis.

> Thrice in her gulf the boiling seas subside,
> Thrice in dire thunders she refunds the tide.

So sang Homer of that then terrifying portent. His account of Charybdis recalls the age when the imaginative Greeks, who were still little more than coasters over summer seas, shrank from the portents of what were to them far-distant waters. Or did not that story originate in the yarns of crafty Phœnician traders who sought to scare these new rivals from their trade route to the West Mediterranean? I shall deal with that question in Chapter ii. Here I note that, despite the assertion of Admiral Smyth, that he had seen a '74 gunship swung round in Charybdis,[1] the modern traveller through the Strait of Messina needs to have the degenerate eddy pointed out to him. The caution to yachtsmen runs in these reassuring terms: "This strait, dreaded by the ancients and invested by them with many imaginary terrors, requires some caution in its navigation on account of the rapidity and irregularity of its currents....Heavy gusts blow down the valleys and gorges".[2] (May not these gusts be the modern counterpart of Homer's Scylla?)

But, for the most part, the Eastern Mediterranean was so calm during half the year (mid-April to mid-

[1] Admiral Smyth, *The Mediterranean*, pp. 178 ff.
[2] *Mediterranean Pilot*, i, 307.

October) as to encourage voyagers even in primitive times. A set of westerly breezes might raise a surface drift and render difficult the weathering of Cape Malea or Mt Athos; or again a squall might now and again blow up and send the rowers scurrying to the nearest land. So uncertain was the sea that you could never be sure of winning the lasting favours of Poseidon. He might be propitiated for a time, but not for long. Such seems to be the inner meaning of Homer's words at the opening of the *Odyssey*. Poseidon has sworn revenge on Odysseus for putting out the eye of Polyphemus. But, when the scene opens, Poseidon is reclining at a pious festival far away in distant Æthiopia, where he accepts the prayers and the hecatombs of oxen long due to him. Therefore there is a calm on the Mediterranean. But in due course Poseidon will return northwards— and then, beware!

One can imagine a Greek of the Hellenistic Age viewing this legend as a naturalistic way of explaining the onrush of the god from the northern waters towards the interior of Africa. When he had passed by there was a calm; and, in due course, there set in a southerly wind—generally moderate—which heralded the return of the deity, more or less appeased and contented.

Such may have been a way of accounting for the spells of calm in the Mediterranean. But Poseidon could break them at will. There were no bounds to

his revenge. Out from a summer sea he, the earth-
shaker, could rear up a giant billow, such as that
which raced roaring landwards to overwhelm Hippo-
lytus and his steeds. That is another legend (surely
arising out of an earthquake wave) which tells of the
inner dread of the Greeks for the unaccountable
element by which they lived. Æschylus might place
in the mouth of Zeus-tortured Prometheus that
moving appeal to "the countless-dimpling smile of
sea waves";[1] but in Greek literature there is no
other outbreak of ecstatic joy in ocean billows such
as pulsates in many a line of Swinburne. Even in that
greatest of sea epics, the *Odyssey*, the sea arouses
thoughts of dread. It is the son of Alcinous, King of
the oar-skilled Phæacians, who declares that "there
is nought else worse than the sea to confound a man,
howsoever hardy he may be".[2] And Odysseus, when
he challenges the Phæacian youth to the sports,
admits that he has been "shamefully broken in many
waters".[3] Thus, even summer voyages were a sore
test of strength, even to a hero; while the crew were
broken down by "toilsome rowing".[4]

As for armies that had to cross the sea they risked
total destruction if Poseidon were angry; and the
Greeks of a later age loved to dwell on his wrath
surging up fiercely against their enemies. For instance, the first Persian armada for the invasion of

[1] Æschylus, *Prometheus*, l. 90.   [2] *Odyssey*, VIII, 138.
[3] *Ibid.* 183, 231.   [4] *Ibid.* x, 78.

Greece was utterly dashed by the blasts of Boreas, which fell on it off Mt Athos and strewed that promontory with 20,000 corpses. Again, ten years later, the far greater armada of Xerxes was shattered by a tempest from the east which fell on it near the base of Mt Pelion. Then 400 ships were dashed to pieces[1]— this, too, in the season of the year fit for sailing. A third storm, even at midsummer, burst upon the large force which he sent round Eubœa to hem in the Greek fleet holding the northern entrance to the Eubœan narrows.[2] But summer storms were rare in the East Mediterranean. It is significant that, when the Greeks were caught by storms in summer they used the term "to be wintered" (χειμα-σθῆναι).

Well was it for the progress of mankind in seamanship that even the Eastern Mediterranean in summer could put men on their mettle. To sail on a sea always as smooth as a duckpond never yet made a seaman. Difficulty and danger, if not overwhelming, have ever developed resourcefulness; and that sea, while not terrifying early man as the Ocean did, early called forth his powers of invention. Though its storms forbade navigation in winter, yet the long spells of calm in summer characteristic of that sea compelled seamen to adopt the best possible means of propulsion then available, that is, the oar. For the carriage of a heavy cargo paddles are of little

---

[1] Herodotus, VI, 44; VII, 188–90.   [2] *Ibid.* VIII, 13.

avail. They may suffice for North American birch-bark canoes or the narrow "outrigger" canoes of the Polynesians, but they cannot propel loads of metal or of tunny far over a sea often beset by summer calms. Surely these climatic conditions must have favoured the substitution of the oar for the paddle.

Another condition favourable to this important change was the existence in Mediterranean lands of forests of pine; for pine yields the long, tough springy poles out of which the best oars can be made. Until man found out the tough and springy nature of the pine, first as mast, secondly as steering paddles, he would probably fail in his experiment of improving on the age-long paddle. But the first ingenious boatman who saw that modified steering paddles might be fastened amidships to serve as propelling oars, made one of the most fruitful discoveries of primitive ages; and I suggest that this is how it may have come about:

Is it not likely that, after long years of paddling, some tired and disgusted paddler would come to the conclusion that pushing the handle-end of the paddle forward with one arm, and using the other hand as a poor kind of fulcrum, was both wearisome and ineffective? And, so soon as that critical paddler fastened the middle part of his paddle to the boat, the thing was half done. Sitting backwards, he could then use both arms to pull and could throw his weight into the work. Then his improved paddle would probably snap and he would fall backwards, amidst the jeers of the other unreflecting paddlers. But, if he were made of the right stuff, he would set about finding wood of the right stuff; and when at last he fashioned a longish pine pole, or oak pole, like a narrower steering oar and worked it in a hole in the side, or fastened it by a thong, he had the laugh on his side.

The change from paddles to oars took place very early in the sea-going ships of Egypt; and it is curious that the artists, in representing early oars, sometimes show the rowers holding them as if they were paddles. But, even so early as the Twelfth Dynasty, crews of thirty rowers are depicted keeping excellent time, probably with oars.[1] Of still earlier date (perhaps 3500 B.C.) is a small silver model of a Babylonian ship fitted with "slender leaf-bladed oars, strangely modern in form".[2]

Whenever and however the oar originated, its chief significance is in the Eastern Mediterranean, probably for the reasons stated above. Early in the Minoan civilization oared ships of a primitive kind are depicted;[3] and it seems likely that the paddle was

---

[1] Torr, C., *Ancient Ships*, p. 2; Chatterton, E., *Sailing Ships*, pp. 34–7.

[2] *Antiquarian Journal*, Oct. 1928, p. 439. See, too, oared ships in Meisner, B., *Babylonien und Assyrien*, I, 250–4.

[3] Evans, *Palace of Cnossus*, I, 17.

superseded by the oar long before the Achæans and Dorians appeared on the scene. So far as I can remember, there is no word for "paddle" in Greek. The Greek ship was always "oared" (ἐπήρετμος); and the verb "to row" (ἐρέσσειν) was used by Æschylus to express the motion of birds with their wings.[1] Now, that motion is down to the horizontal, not further down to the vertical; so it resembles the work of the oar, not that of the paddle, which is vertical. My conjecture, that the substitution of the oar for the paddle belongs to pre-Greek times, is strengthened by a passage in Arrian's *Indica*[2] (xxvii, 4). He there describes the Greeks during the voyage of Nearchus arriving at Kophes harbour:

> There fishermen dwelt and they had small and bad boats; and they rowed with their oars (τῆσι κώπησιν), not by using a thole-pin (as is the custom of Greeks), but as it were throwing the water in the river here and there (ἔνθεν καὶ ἔνθεν), just as diggers throw the earth.

This interesting passage breathes the contempt of good oarsmen (who of course do not "dig") for wretched boatmen who had no thole-pins, and did dig, with much splashing, and apparently little progress. The well-oared Greeks despised those clumsy fellows, who obviously were using paddles. The Greeks learnt about seacraft from the

[1] Æschylus, *Agamemnon*, l. 52.
[2] Written about A.D. 150; it describes the voyage of Nearchus as a supplement to his *Anabasis of Alexander*.

Minoans, or, later, from the Phœnicians, both of whom certainly used oars.

In the next chapter we shall consider that strange and secretive people, the Phœnicians. But, here, in connection with the topic of timber and shipbuilding, we may note that they had greater advantages than the Assyrians, Egyptians, or indeed than most of the Greeks. For near Sidon and Tyre was the Lebanon with forests of cedar, oak, pine, etc. So skilled did the Phœnicians become in felling and moving great timber that Solomon bargained with Hiram, King of Tyre, that he should send his skilled foresters to hew cedars and firs for the building of the Jewish temple; and the timber was conveyed by sea on floats from Tyre to Joppa.[1] Ability to fell large trees and use them for construction was one of the factors making for the early maritime supremacy of the Phœnicians; and probably their skill in utilizing the forests of Lebanon gained them pre-eminence in shipbuilding over the Egyptians.[2] At any rate, it seems certain that the Egyptians, after their two naval victories, of about 1190 B.C., over the "peoples of the sea", underwent a period of

---

[1] 1 Kings v.
[2] On the lack of good timber in Egypt see Köster, p. 13. Is it not likely also that the traditional build of the Egyptian river-boat too much influenced that of their sea-going ships? The Phœnicians had to make good sea-going ships straightway.

decline, which sapped their seafaring activities;[1] while about then the Phœnicians came to the fore. In the same period the Minoan power in Crete, which had planted the vigorous Philistine offshoot at Gaza, was on the wane,[2] perhaps owing to a succession of severe earthquakes, followed by invasions. But is it not possible that the Minoans had to some extent depleted their forests, and thus impaired their ship-building power?

I venture to suggest that the naval power of the Mediterranean peoples depended largely on the proximity of forests of suitable timber. The supply of wood must be considerable; for at any great emergency a fleet might be wanted quickly, and wholesale building implies a large reserve of fairly seasoned timber. Further, in early times when roads were mere rough tracks, the proximity of forests to the chief harbour was a great asset for shipbuilding.

Is it not also likely that the catalogue of ships in the *Iliad* (Bk II) registers roughly the presumed shipbuilding capacity of the early Greek States? The Greek armada which sailed against Troy is reckoned at 1183 ships—an impossible number. For how could a force of something like 100,000 warriors and oarsmen possibly be fed on that narrow and barren plain unless they caught a shoal of big tunny every other day? The storms of autumn and winter pre-

[1] *Camb. Ancient Hist.* II, 172–5.
[2] Evans, *Palace of Cnossus*, II, 287.

cluded all hope of succour in provisions during nearly half of the year. Nevertheless the numbers of the different contingents enable us to gauge the relative strength of the Greek cities which sent forces against Troy. Thus, 100 ships sailed from Mycenæ, and 90 from Elis; 80 came alike from Argos and Crete, and 60 from Lacedæmon and Arcadia; while Athens, Bœotia and Thessaly sent only 50 apiece; and so on. These numbers seem to represent the presumed ship-building capacity of the Greek States at the time of the Trojan War;[1] and it is also noteworthy that extensive mountainous areas like Mycenæ, Elis, Argos and Crete contributed the largest numbers, while Athens sent only 50 ships. This last was about the natural quota for Athens, seeing that she had not then acquired political power, and was situated in a country poor in large timber. On the other hand the numbers from Crete, viz. 80, show that that island had regained something of the naval power which made her mistress of the East Mediterranean in the Early and Middle Minoan Ages. Nature has marked out parts of that island as forest land; and its timber supply would far surpass that of the whole of Attica, whose pre-eminence at sea was always precarious because she depended largely on other areas for suitable timber.

[1] See Allen, T. W., *The Catalogue of the Greek Ships*. Ridgeway, Sir W., in *The Early Age of Greece*, pp. 109, 607, places the Homeric poems before 1000 B.C.

When, therefore, we study the maritime history of ancient States we should remember their dependence on the supply of timber in regions where forests were not very extensive, besides being subject to fires and the destructive nibbling of goats. Indeed, the fall of some States may have resulted from the exhaustion of their forests. Thus, the decline of Tyre and Sidon was probably due to their increasing difficulty in getting timber from Lebanon and Mt Hermon so soon as the neighbouring great monarchies held their hinterland. And may not the perplexing collapse of the sea power of Carthage have resulted from her inability to procure enough large timber for shipbuilding after she lost Sicily, Sardinia and Corsica to the Romans?

Shipbuilding depends not only on timber but also on metals. What, then, was the supply of metals in the Mediterranean lands? Herein the conditions were less favourable, especially in the East. Copper was plentiful in Cyprus (whence the metal has its name), also in some of the Cyclades, and it was worked even in early times largely for the needs of the Egyptians, Assyrians and Babylonians. Indeed, it is likely that the early workers of metals made their first long voyages in the Mediterranean in order to gain supplies of copper.[1] And the Phœni-

[1] See *Camb. Ancient Hist.* I, 90, for the use of the valued copper of Cyprus.

cians probably gained wealth and power by furnish-
ing metals to the great land empires. Copper also
figures largely in the life of the early Greeks; for
instance, in the *Odyssey* (Bk i) Athena comes in the
guise of a shipman carrying a cargo of shining iron
to barter with copper from Mt Temesa (or Tamasia)
in Cyprus.

Copper alone is too soft and pliable to make good
nails, still less weapons. When, however, copper is
mixed with tin, the alloy, bronze, is far harder, and
is capable of taking a good edge. Hence the incoming
of bronze (the "man-exalting bronze" of Homer)[1]
marks a step forward in human progress. Even by
2000 B.C. the mixture of one part tin to nine of
copper was "the standard combination".[2] Thenceforth, or perhaps earlier, voyages to the West for
tin became imperative; for there is no tin in the
East Mediterranean; and the nearest sources of
supply for seamen were in Tuscany and North-west
Spain—sources far from large and now exhausted.
Cornwall was far richer in tin, and, despite its re-
moteness from the Levant, probably sent thither no
small quantity even from very early times, chiefly
to be worked up into bronze weapons or armour but

---

[1] εὐήνωρ (in *Odyssey*, XIII, 19).

[2] Childe, *The Bronze Age*, p. 7. See, too, p. 51 for the statement "No true ships certainly antedate the copper axe and
chisel". He traces trade in metals between Troy II and
Bohemia.

also for shipbuilding. Though oak pegs were often used for fastenings, yet bronze nails were preferred as being sharper and not liable to shrink, while they excelled iron as not rusting.[1] For these and other reasons tin was greatly prized. Probably its acquisition furnished the chief motive prompting the early inhabitants of the East Mediterranean to undertake long voyages to the West. And it is long voyaging which has always developed seacraft.

The same remark applies, though in a lesser degree, to the acquisition of iron; for, with the exception of small deposits in Cyprus, this metal is rare in the East Mediterranean, but less so in the western part of that sea. A larger source of supply for shipmen was found in the island of Ilva (Elba), where it was worked in early times, e.g. by the Etruscans. They were then, and long after, keen rivals of the Phœnicians. So it is doubtful whether these last got their supplies of iron from Ilva through the Etruscans. More probably they relied on the still larger stores of iron which were early discovered in the hills of Pontus, east of the River Iris. The tribe of the Chalybes worked up this iron, whence the

[1] Vegetius, *De Re militari*, ch. 4: Fawns, S., *Tin Deposits of the World*, pp. 5 ff., 145, shows that the Spanish supply of tin was small. Large bronze nails and studs have been found on the Roman galleys in Lake Nemi. On the other hand the Roman ship found in the Thames mud near London (and now in the London Museum) is fastened together by wooden pegs.

Greeks called the refined metal χάλυψ.[1] As the deposits were near the Euxine, the Greeks probably obtained their iron thence by ships, through the Bosporus and Hellespont. Larger stores may have reached the Ægean by the same route from the still more extensive iron deposits further east in Armenia. In the Homeric Age iron tools began to replace those of bronze; so did iron anchors those of bronze or stone, only to be superseded by leaden ones. But at that time iron was to be had only in small quantities. Thus, Achilles offered a lump of iron as one of the prizes at the funeral games of Patroclus, and incited the heroes to hurl the lump; for it would supply the victor with ploughshares, wheels and other necessaries of the farm.[2] Bronze, however, still remained the favourite metal for weapons.[3]

Enough has been said to show that the paucity of iron in the East Mediterranean spurred on seamen to discover lands where that metal could be procured. Indeed, without iron, tin and copper, man could not effectively plough the land, make war, or construct a serviceable ship. Also it is obvious that progress in shipbuilding depended largely on skill in metal work (especially bronze and iron) for the making of bronze nails and fastenings and iron anchors.

[1] See Xenophon, *Anabasis*, v, 5.
[2] *Iliad*, XXIII, 826–35.
[3] Lang, A., *The World of Homer*, ch. 10.

But this is only a small part of the shipwright's task. More fundamental still is the discovery of suitable woods for the keel, the planking, the mast, the yard, and the oars of a ship. Man must have striven long before he learnt to plane planks accurately, to fasten them together, first with withies, or, later, with nails or pegs, and to calk them; then to erect the mast firmly in its socket and support it with ropes of cowhide or, later, of flax or hemp; then to weave the sails of flax or papyrus, or else sew oxhides together. Many must have been the experiments with oars, especially the broader steering oars (miscalled rudders); and great was the triumph when some inventive brain devised an outer quasi-fulcrum for oars (ἐπεξειρεσία), which increased the leverage in rowing without necessarily extending the beam of the vessel. Finally there came the never-ending problem of shaping the hull so that it would rise to the waves, and not overturn in the trough of the sea. All this must have taken many centuries of experimenting; and until man had made some progress in all the mechanical arts he stood helpless on shore—or went to the bottom.

I have referred earlier to the fertilizing contacts which took place where land and sea most intermingled. Obviously, such contacts were most numerous and fruitful in great archipelagos like that of the Ægean Sea. For there, as will appear in due course, Nature distributed her gifts very diversely

among the different isles;[1] and man, unable to live
in comfort on the products of any one of them, had to
trade with several. He fared best who bartered most
widely. Thus, the Ægean peoples early developed a
culture which, when quickened by admixture with
the manly Achæans and Dorians of the North, far
excelled that of the more stereotyped civilizations
of the Nile, Euphrates and Tigris. The sea is the
most potent mixer, whether of peoples, products or
thoughts; and the people which emerges from its
stirrings and buffetings becomes both strong and
receptive. Like the Ithaca of Odysseus, the Ægean
world was "a good nurse of heroes".[2]

Above all, that microcosm existed and developed
by seacraft; and its scions made no secret of the
means which they had devised or learnt from others.
In the Homeric poems is outlined the story of the
early Greek ship. Look at the earliest description
we have of the building of a primitive boat,[3] viz.
that of Odysseus, and note the tools which, at the
behest of the gods, the goddess-nymph, Calypso,
reluctantly gave him. They were merely a great
bronze double-edged axe for felling the trees of her
isle of Ogygia, viz. alder, poplar and heaven-high

---

[1] See comments on those insular diversities in the *Hymn
to Apollo*, ll. 43–68.

[2] *Odyssey*, IX, 27.

[3] See Brewster, F., on "The Raft of Odysseus" in *Harvard
Studies in Classical Philology* (1926), pp. 49 ff.

pine; and of them he felled twenty. Then with a polished adze he made from them planks which he smoothed and fashioned true to line. Meanwhile Calypso fetched augers for boring; and he made holes in the planks and fastened them together with "bolts and joins". He now fashioned his craft broad at the bottom, somewhat like a raft, and on it he set up the deckings, fitting them to the close-set uprights. In the deckings he set up the mast and fitted to it a yard-arm, and made a steering oar for guiding his craft. The whole he fenced with wattled osier, backed with wood, so as to keep out the waves. Then Calypso brought him web of cloth; and out of it he wove a sail; and on to the mast and the yard he bound braces, halyards and reefing-sheets.[1]

At last, on the fourth day (so Homer says), Odysseus pushed his vessel with levers down to the sea. On the fifth Calypso sent a fair wind which wafted him away; and he sat, guiding the craft with his steering oar. Warding off sleep from his eyelids, he sat still all night, keeping on his left the constellation of the Great Bear, "which alone hath no part in the baths of the Ocean". And thus, on the 18th day he saw ahead the land of the Phæacians, when, lo, Poseidon fresh back from Æthiopia, saw him and dashed his frail craft to pieces.[2]

Such is the first detailed account we have of boat-building and boat-sailing by one man alone. Of

[1] *Odyssey*, v, 230–61.   [2] *Ibid*. v, 282–96.

course Calypso supplied the bronze or iron tools and the web for the sail; and those tools and that web imply centuries of work and exploration. Surely, when one man could make a boat in four days and sail the Mediterranean during seventeen days and nights, the first supremely difficult step had been taken towards conquering the sea. But is it not equally certain that only the Mediterranean could supply the *milieu* for working this miracle?

For an account of a fast and well-found ship we may again turn to Homer. In the *Odyssey* he shows us how far the shipwrights of Ithaca had succeeded in making such a craft. Look at the swift ship of Ithaca which Athena, disguised as a shipman, secured for the voyage of Telemachus. Ithaca's seamen were bold and skilful. They came readily at the call of Telemachus, and Athena saw to it that the decked ship was stored with all necessaries. There were stowed on board 12 great jars of wine, also 20 measures of the grain of bruised barley meal. Then the goddess and Telemachus went on board and sat in the stern; while she "sent them a favourable gale, a fresh west wind, singing over the wine-dark sea.... So they raised the mast of pine tree and set it in the hole of the cross plank, and made it fast with fore-stays, and hauled up the white sails with twisted ropes of oxhide. And the wind filled the belly of the sail; and the dark wave seethed loudly round the stem of the running ship, and she fleeted over the wave".[1]

[1] *Odyssey*, ii, 420–9.

So sped the ship onward, night and day; for the goddess breathed on them the favouring wind that bore them by the next dawn to sandy Pylos. That was an ideal voyage. No need was there for the 20 rowers to toil with the oar against a head wind; and no need to follow the deep winding coasts of islands and mainland; for the goddess-sent breeze full astern wafted them straight across the open sea to their landfall.

Very different was the hard reality to the average sailor. The calms usual in summer compelled him to toil with the oar under the fierce sun; and rarely did he trust himself far from shore; for thirst alone would bid him turn to coves where streams might be found. Greek wine was not thirst-quenching, rather heating. So, if only for the assuaging of thirst, the Greeks kept near the shore, and if possible always slept on shore. By this plan they also avoided the breezes which often ruffled the deep early and late in the day.

An example of their longing for the night's rest ashore is found in the opposition offered to Odysseus at sundown soon after they had passed the rock of Scylla. They were nearing the dread island where grazed the sacred oxen of the Sun; and the sweet sound of lowing oxen was heard. Yet Odysseus sought to get the crew past the island by night, though the heart of his men was broken within them by toil and grief. Thereupon Eurylochus (the Jack Deadeye of the crew) upbraided him with sheer sweating of his men: "Hardy art thou, Odysseus, of might beyond measure, and thy limbs are never weary; verily thou art fashioned all of iron, thou that sufferest not thy fellows, foredone with toil and drowsiness, to set foot on shore, where we might presently prepare us a good supper in this sea-girt island. But, even as we are, thou biddest us fare blindly through the sudden night and from the isle go wandering on the misty deep. And strong winds, the bane of ships, are born in the night ".[1]

Jack Deadeye's eloquence, backed by the prospect of a good supper ashore, carries the day hopelessly against the master. And so there is a general strike against him—a strike for a twelve-hour day afloat and probably twelve hours ashore, where there is a gurgling stream, not to speak of sea nymphs ready to welcome them. We sympathize with the men; but Homer does not. For their sacrilege in slaying the sacred oxen of the Sun he drowns them all by the thunderbolt of Zeus. Even pious Odysseus barely escapes on the mast which Charybdis opportunely throws up, and he then has a nine days' swim and paddle for dear life. At the end of the tenth day he reaches the island of the goddess-nymph, Calypso, who detains him seven years.

Voyaging in the Mediterranean was then full of weird contrasts. Sharp trials alternated with long spells of Sybaritic repose. But that is exactly the life which the true seaman loves.

[1] *Odyssey*, xii, 279–87.

CHAPTER II

GRÆCO-PHŒNICIAN RIVALRIES

The blending and the distribution of early races over the Mediterranean is far too vast a subject for treatment here; we can but sketch its salient features and try to explain its chief crises. Let us therefore limit our inquiry to the rivalries of the two chief seafaring peoples of historic times, the Greeks and Phœnicians. I decline to enter the Minoan and Etruscan mazes. But it may be granted that Minoan seamen preceded the Phœnicians in long-distance voyages into the Western Mediterranean.[1]

Scholars in general are agreed that the Hellenes, or Greeks, were a composite people, formed on the basis of the primitive Ægean or Helladic stock by successive admixtures of northern invaders, especially the Achæans and, later, the Dorians. If this be so, the older and relatively civilized inhabitants of Greece, of its islands and the west of Asia Minor, underwent an infusion of northern blood which probably exercised an invigorating influence physically, though it may, for a time at least, have set back the slow march of the old order.[2]

There are signs that the invaders knew little or

[1] On the earliest sea powers see Burn, A. R., *Minoans, Philistines, Greeks*.

[2] *Ibid.* chap. x for details; also Cary and Warmington, *The Ancient Explorers*, chap. II.

nothing about the sea; and it is significant that Achæans are represented by Homer as scorning a fish diet, which was for the poor folk. But it seems probable that the earlier sea-dwellers of the Ægean transmitted most of their maritime qualities to the conquerors of what is a sea-girt microcosm. And I would suggest that the Hellenic compound owed its unrivalled qualities to the fine stuff of which the blend was composed and of its suitability to that glorious habitat. Undeniably, the union put a new edge on the energies of the older sea-traders and also lured the landsmen on to the element which has always made for love of freedom and adventure.

Hellas, then, is land-born but also sea-born; and it is possible to detect in her two great epics the inspiriting dualism of her origins. For surely the *Iliad* is the typical offspring of her older clan life on land. That poem depicts the military prowess of the Achæans when put to the utmost test by a call of honour to action overseas. Only to avenge the rape of a queen would all those chieftains have launched their armada to lay low the walls of Troy. The whole enterprise tells of the long effort of conquering soldiers who detest the sea yet are resolved to sack the fortress of those perfidious sea-raiders. Achilles and the other Greek leaders are essentially feudal chiefs whose actions and motives are dictated by an intense though narrow code of chivalry. The setting of the poem is Greek. Egypt, the pygmies of

Æthiopia, and the stream of Oceanus are only dimly known; and, if I mistake not, there are in the *Iliad* only two references to Phœnicians. The whole crusade is national and military, alien in spirit to the commercial *motif* which modern scholiasts have tried to read into its cause. Even at the end of that ten years' war, the heroes do not know the best way back to Greece. They split up in doubt at Tenedos; and those who reach Lesbos ponder about the long voyage, and finally sacrifice many thighs of bulls to Poseidon when they reach the southern tip of Eubœa, and doubtless many more when, on the fourth day, they beach their craft at Argos.

Far different is the spirit of the *Odyssey*. In it one snuffs on every page the tang of the sea. Though the fundamental theme is the home-coming of Odysseus, yet how skilfully is that *dénouement* delayed! For, in the *Odyssey*, the sea spirit is paramount. The setting also is no longer only national, it is Mediterranean. Nay, it includes the stream of Oceanus and the land of the Cimmerians, ever "shrouded in mist and cloud"; and there Homer places the entrance to Hades,[1] where his hero seeks to plumb the mysteries of the other world. Oceanus also links on with the Mediterranean—a good guess —and with the Caspian and Euxine—a bad guess. Egypt, Sicily, Ithaca, and probably also Corfu, are referred to with fair accuracy.

[1] *Odyssey*, xi, 15.

Indeed, the Greek mind, now awake to the wonder of the outer world, is here seen aflame with curiosity. In the land of the Cyclopes Odysseus, unlike his tired and discontented oarsmen, longs to find out "what manner of folk they are, whether froward and wild and unjust, or hospitable and of God-fearing mind".[1] So he persists in his novel quest. He knows it to be dangerous, but he goes on, armed with his own mother wit and a skin of strong wine—to meet the monster Cyclops! A fool, you will say. Yes; but his "lordly mind" is spurred on by a curiosity which scorns all sense of danger. He is no longer the half-timid chieftain of the *Iliad*, remarkable only for cunning, and once at least for skulking by the ships. Now he is the almost reckless explorer; for even after the Polyphemus episode he risks himself among the Læstrygonians and on Circe's isle to find out the ways of strange men; "for a strong constraint is laid on me".[2] It is this zest for the unknown which is the glory of the *Odyssey*, as it was to be the glory of the Greeks in diverse spheres of life. Andrew Lang has thus sung of that first and greatest of all epics of adventure:

> So, gladly from the songs of modern speech
> Men turn, and see the stars, and feel the free
> Shrill wind beyond the close of heavy flowers,
> And through the music of the languid hours
> They hear, like ocean on a western beach,
> The surge and thunder of the *Odyssey*.

[1] *Odyssey*, IX, 173–5.   [2] *Ibid*. x, 269.

The poem breathes the ineffable charm of the childhood of the race blossoming into the curiosity of youth; for the Homeric Age then hovered on the verge of a new world, far beyond Hellas and the Ægean—a new world of marvels that beckoned forward every daring voyager. Had it not been half revealed and half concealed by the men of Sidon and Tyre? And did not those seamen draw their wealth thence? What wonder that the Phœnicians figure largely in the *Odyssey*, so that an able Frenchman has regarded them as the concealed prompters of all its thaumaturgy. Of that theory more in the sequel. Here I note merely that Homer's references to them are unfavourable. They are "famous sailors, greedy merchantmen, with countless gauds in a black ship".[1] In short, they are cheaters of men and tempters of women; and therein he set the fashion for all time.

Greek writers and indeed all Greeks had an instinctive dislike of those swarthy Semites, who were before them in all waters. Unwillingly those pioneers of commerce had half-opened up the way for others to strange lands rich in tin, silver, iron and amber. But, like all early sea-traders, they kept their routes and methods secret. And this is not surprising; for the cargoes of early ships were small and the dangers for mariners incredibly great. Naturally, then, the best seamen of the ancient world sought to establish and retain a monopoly in articles which were coveted

[1] *Odyssey*, xv, 415–22.

by every queen, every warrior, every farmer. Egypt
and Crete from the time of their decline, and Greece
in the dawn of her new vigour, alike needed these
and other articles for ornaments, weapons and tools.
So, during several centuries, the men of Sidon and
Tyre were almost the only sea-traffickers in cloths,
metals and amber. Fishing and other local trades
could be carried on by any coasters; but it is one
thing to fish in a bay, or coast along the shore,
landing at dusk for supper and sleep, after the way
of Eurylochus; and quite another thing to push out
into the vast unknown, find your way by the stars
at night, and persevere for weeks, perhaps months,
until you reach the head of the Adriatic or Euxine,
or breast the tides of Oceanus beyond the Pillars of
Hercules. During long ages, by comparison with
which British maritime supremacy is a mushroom
growth, the sailors of Sidon and Tyre plied their
tasks in mere cockle shells, and brought home the
silver and fruits of Tarshish, the tin of North-west
Spain (some say also of Cornwall), the corn of Gaul,
Sardinia, and North Africa, the Baltic amber carried
overland to the Adriatic, the fish, corn, iron and
caravan produce of the Levant.

Is it surprising that these sea lords, able to find
their way across broad waters without starving,
should claim and practise a monopoly in all distant
treasures? The sole long-distance voyagers of every
age, from the Phœnicians to the Dutch, have acted in

much the same way. The argument is cogent—"If you want Cornish tin in the Ægean, or the cloves of the Spice Islands in West Europe, we defy you to fetch them". In truth, the only way to beat the long-distance monopolists is to beat them in long-distance voyaging. And this supreme triumph of seacraft came about slowly in the ancient world.

How could it be otherwise? In that world the sea was the abode of violence. Early man was more apt to clutch at present and easy gain by plundering or kidnapping than to toil far into the unknown for a doubtful and remote profit. Ages of rapine and consequent poverty had to pass before he acquired that longer view which is the guiding star of commerce. Even in Homer's time it gave no offence to ask a stranger "Are you a pirate?"; and Thucydides in his far-distant age noted that of yore all sea-trading took place under the shadow of fear.[1] His sage remark is borne out by the sites of the earliest cities. Scarcely one of them is on the coast. Nearly all seek the defence of a hill or acropolis some distance inland. The Minoan capitals, Cnossus and Phæstus, were built some five miles from the barter posts on the shore. So too, Mycenæ, Troy, Athens, Corinth, practically every city of early times, shunned the coast and sought some defensible position inland. The corresponding trading post was generally a peninsula where a treacherous onrush could be fore-

[1] Thucydides, 1, 2.

seen, as at the Phœnician post, occupied later, called by the Greeks Heracles Monoikos (Monaco); or else still better, it was an island or islands near the mainland. Sometimes these islands, or even posts on an open shore, were placed under a kind of perpetual truce; or else exchange went on without the parties actually meeting.[1] Examples of coastal islets used for trade were Sidon, Tyre and the Pharos (all originally separate from the mainland); also (I believe) the island north of Candia for Cnossus; the islets off the Piræus, Phocæa, Miletus, Massilia; and Ortygia (the nucleus of Syracuse). It is probable that trade on these and many other islets long preceded trade on the mainland near by.

Note also that early traffickers avoided narrow inlets like the Piræus for fear of being cut off. Dread of treachery in an enclosed creek lies at the heart of the Læstrygonian legend of the *Odyssey*.[2] All but one of the ships of Odysseus had rowed right into a narrow cliff-bound cleft, but he himself, before setting about his ethnic quest, cautiously tied up his craft to a rock at the entrance. Result: all the other boats' crews were overwhelmed by stones and then eaten, while the explorer himself fled to his boat, severed the rope with his sword and escaped with his men. Moral: don't trust strangers who live around

[1] Rose, H. J., *Early Culture in Greece*, p. 227.
[2] *Odyssey*, x, 87–132; Bérard, V., *Les Phéniciens et l'Odyssée*, I, 178–81.

a natural death-trap, but trust the calm of the Mediterranean summer rather than the changeful moods of strange men. Such a feeling prompted the choice of an open bay rather than a narrow creek, as appeared in the preference accorded to Phalerum Bay over the Piræus right down to the time of Salamis.

Slave-raiding or kidnapping was a common by-product of ancient commerce. In fact, Herodotus strikes the keynote of his history of the long war between Greece and Persia in the very first scene, which shows Phœnician traders backing their ships on the shore near Argos and displaying their wares for some days. At last come Argive women, tempted by the glitter, whereupon the swarthy seamen rush upon them, hurry them on ship and sail away with would-be customers suddenly become slaves. If, however, the uncommunicative Phœnicians had left behind any records they would doubtless have told of similar abductions of women by the worshippers of Zeus.

Such being the conditions of early sea trade, was it not natural that Phœnicians and Greeks should become keen rivals? Consider also their habitats. Somewhere about 2800 B.C. the Phœnicians migrated from the shores of the Erythræan Sea to the coast of what came to be called Syria. Such was their tradition, passed on to Herodotus.[1] Other authorities

[1] Herodotus, II, 44; Fleming, W. B., *Hist. of Tyre*, pp. 3–5.

trace them back to the shores of the Persian Gulf. Or, again, they may be autochthonous. In any case they were a seafaring people, who formed their chief cities, Sidon and Tyre, on two islets very near a coast to which caravans brought the produce of the East. Probably their precursors had already built up a maritime trade;[1] but the Phœnicians greatly extended it. As we have seen, the northerly current which flows along the Syrian coast favoured the run towards Asia Minor or Cyprus: also their coast was rich in the *murex* which produced the purple dye so much prized for the working up of their fabrics;[2] and doubtless the caravan trade from the East favoured the growth of an export trade, even if it did not prompt their original settlement on those islets. Also not far from the coast was the great forest of Lebanon, rich in timber for shipbuilding. Naturally, then, the Phœnicians became the chief, almost the sole, middlemen, between East and West.

Their trafficking spirit soon brought friction between them and their cousins, the Hebrews. These, when settled on the hilly ground to the south-east became a pastoral or agricultural people, landlocked and introspective, while the sea-girt Phœnicians grew to be the boldest seamen and the keenest exploiters of the early world. A phrase which I shall

[1] For details see Baron von Landau in *Der alte Orient* for 1901, pp. 6–8.
[2] Strabo, xvi, 2–23.

quote presently from Ezekiel shows that Tyre and Sidon may have competed with Jerusalem for the eastern caravan trade. Also it is symptomatic that Nehemiah lifted up his voice against Phœnician traders for daring to sell fish in Jerusalem on the Jewish Sabbath.[1]

The monopolist trader always draws on himself dislike, even of those who are fain to buy his wares. But if he alone can bring valued articles, and can deftly grovel, his trade will grow. Egyptian sculptures show Phœnician traders kneeling as they offer tribute or blackmail to the Pharaohs for permission to trade; for, as we saw in Chapter I, the men of Tyre and Sidon began to absorb the sea-borne trade of Egypt about 1150 B.C.,[2] just as, somewhat earlier, they succeeded the Cretans as lords of the Eastern Mediterranean.

Truly, if any men were compelled to become daring seamen and expert bargainers, it was those of Sidon and Tyre. Living between the devil (Nebuchadnezzar, or his like) and the deep sea, they shunned the former and wooed the latter. Their sea risks were their salvation. Unlike the men of the Nile they had no riverine apprenticeship. No easy voyaging for the Phœnicians! Once out of their narrow harbours, they faced the open Mediterranean, with no shelter nearer than Cyprus. For them sea-

[1] Nehemiah xiii, 16.
[2] Köster, *Das antike Seewesen*, p. 48.

faring was a case of sink or swim. What wonder that
they became skilful seamen, scorning to hug the
coast like Greeks of the Ægean, holding on their
course by the help of the stars to the bounds of the
then known world? How they lasted out to the end
we shall never know; for they left the telling of
seamen's tales to the talkative Greeks. Though
Greek tradition credits them (perhaps wrongly)
with inventing the alphabet, yet very few of their
writings are extant. At least, no story of a Phœnician voyage survives except that of Hanno.[1] Secretly,
as was their wont, they toiled to and fro over the
Mediterranean, founding their trading posts in the
southern Greek islets like Cerigo, then further on
in Malta and Pantelleria; then at Utica, later at
Carthage, also in Sicily, Sardinia, Corsica; finally at
Monaco and Pyrene. Even outside the Mediterranean, amidst those swirling tides, which terrified
everyone else, they forged ahead, and on an island
founded Gades (Cadiz), the mother city of Atlantic
commerce. In Southern Spain (Tarshish) they procured fruits and silver in abundance; and they
brought back stores of the precious metal, to work it
up into ornaments; for Jeremiah writes—"Silver
spread into plates is brought from Tarshish, and
gold from Uphaz".[2] Whether they ventured across
the Bay of Biscay to the Cassiterides, there to

[1] For this see Cary and Warmington, pp. 47–52.
[2] Jeremiah x, 9,.

bargain with Cornishmen for the tin of Cornwall, is doubtful. Cargoes of tin consort ill with the billows of the Bay of Biscay in times of relatively small galleys propelled chiefly by oars. The Cornish enthusiasm which clings to the Phœnician legend is lovable; but I confess my scepticism. Nor am I converted by the charming addition that the recipe for making true Cornish cream has a Phœnician origin.

That Cornish tin made its way to South Europe is undoubted; but that fact does not necessarily imply its carriage across the mouth of the English Channel and of the Bay of Biscay; also the coasting of that bay is exceedingly dangerous. On naval grounds, then, and in default of decisive evidence, I decline to believe that Cornish tin was regularly brought over the Atlantic; for that ocean is often so cloudy that the Phœnicians, who found their way by the stars, would be baffled and lose their way. It seems far more probable that the Cassiterides were the Bayona Isles off Galicia, where tin was then found in abundance. We must also remember that the carriage of metallic ores was fraught with danger even in the usually placid Mediterranean. Such is surely the significance of the statement of Ezekiel that the east wind broke the ships of Tarshish in the midst of the seas, which may be paralleled by that of the Psalmist —"Thou breakest the ships of Tarshish with an east wind".[1] Why this insistence on an east wind as

[1] Ezekiel xxvii, 26; Psalm xlviii, 7.

so fatal? Assuredly because on their return voyage to
Tyre or Sidon they would be heavily laden with the
silver and tin of Tarshish. Can we, then, believe
that even the relatively large "ships of Tarshish"
(compare our term "East Indiamen") would, when
laden with Cornish tin, weather the Biscay storms?
I do not; though of course single ships may oc-
casionally have done so. It seems far more probable
that the regular route for Cornish tin would be by
way of the Straits of Dover, then to the south of
Gaul by way of the Rhone Valley, and so to the
Levant.

For a life-like account of Tyre and the Tyrians we
must go to a hostile witness, the prophet Ezekiel,
about 600 B.C. He denounces Tyrus because she
rejoiced over the woes of Jerusalem, "that was the
gates of the people"—perhaps a sign of the trade
rivalry between Tyre and Jerusalem. In significant
words he foretells the overthrow of Tyre by Nebuchadnezzar: "How art thou destroyed, that wast inhabited of seafaring men, the renowned city, which
wast strong in the sea, she and all her inhabitants,
which cause their terror to be on all that haunt it".
He then describes her as "a merchant of the people
unto many isles": her ships were made of fir trees
of Senir (Mt Hermon); her masts were from the
cedars of Lebanon; her oars were fashioned from the
oaks of Bashan (east of Jordan), the benches of her
ships were of ivory from the Isles of Chittim. Linen

from Egypt provided her with sails: "Thy wise men, O Tyrus, were thy pilots: and the old men of Gebal were thy calkers. They of Persia and of Lud and of Phut were in thine army, thy men of war"— "Tarshish was thy merchant by reason of the multitude of all kind of riches; with silver, iron, tin and lead they traded for thy wares. Javan, Tubal and Meshech were thy traffickers: they traded the persons of men and vessels of brass for thy merchandize".[1] Ezekiel then says that the isles of the sea, as well as Syria, Damascus, Judah, Israel, Arabia, Sheba, Eden, brought to Tyre their riches in precious stones, wool, cloths, corn, wine, cattle, sheep and goats: "The ships of Tarshish were thy caravans for thy merchandize, and thou wast replenished and made very glorious in the midst of the seas". But then (v. 26) comes the woe: "Thy rowers have brought thee into great waters: the east wind hath broken thee in the midst of the seas". So that all who handle the oar shall lament over thee, saying: "Who is there like Tyre, like her that is brought to silence in the midst of the sea"? "The merchants among the peoples shall hiss at thee: thou art become a terror, and never shalt be any more".[2]

It lay in the nature of things that these long-distance traffickers, these jealous monopolists, should clash with the Greeks, whose islands lay across the

[1] Ezekiel xxvi, xxvii.   [2] *Ibid.*

Phœnician routes to Gades, the West Mediterranean and the Euxine. For the Greeks depended
on Ægean trade just as much as their eastern rivals
depended on trade beyond the Ægean. In fact, the
Ægean microcosm forms an interdependent whole,
lacking the useful metals but possessing the other
requisites of early civilization. Thus, Naxos contained emery; Melos, obsidian; Chios, Paros and
Melos supplied marble; while Rhodes, Cos, Chios
and Samos were remarkable for their fertility and
exported wine, fruit, grain, and pottery. The poor
soil of many parts of Greece made them partly dependent on the islands; and those Greek cities prospered most, both materially and culturally, which
traded most freely with the islands. Athens in her
palmiest days boasted of her glad acceptance of
foreign produce[1]—a habit, based primarily on open
trading with the Ægean, which made for the primacy
of the city of the violet crown.

An expansive people like the Greeks naturally
challenged the close control of its outlying islets
exercised by the Phœnicians. Indeed, the friction
between the two peoples, beginning on the fringe of
the Greek world, was certain to become a clash of
two opposing trade systems, that of comparatively
free-dealing coasters with monopolist long-distance
seamen passing through a Greek archipelago. And
such clashes became more frequent and severe when

[1] Thucydides, II, 38.

the fertile Hellenes spread their colonies overseas far into the Phœnician preserves, westwards into Sicily and South Italy, and southwards into Libya. There the promise of the Delphic oracle, that 100 Greek cities would be founded, remained un-fulfilled. But a colony sent out from Thera about 630 B.C. found a favourable site at Cyrene, where trade soon increased with tribes of the interior.[1] Thus grew by degrees the Cyrenaica, an important centre of Greek influence and a barrier to the eastern extension of that of Carthage.

Græco-Phœnician friction in the Western Medi-terranean we shall discuss later. Here we are con-cerned rather with that which arose in the straits leading to the Euxine. Very early the Greeks pressed up those straits, perhaps, first, after the tunny. The colonizing enterprise of Miletus was especially re-markable. So early as 770 B.C. she founded Sinope in the Euxine and, soon after, Trapezus, so as to get a full share of the iron of Pontus, also of the caravan trade from Persia.

Now, mastery of the Euxine depended on mastery of the straits leading to that sea. Indeed, the history of seas is largely the history of the Narrows which lead to them; and of all straits, the Bosporus and Hellespont are by far the most important. We may go further and say that the mastery of seas lies in the mastery of the straits which lead to them. That of

[1] Herodotus, IV, 156, 179.

the Mediterranean centres largely in the Hellespont, Bosporus, and the Straits of Messina and Gibraltar. That is doubtless the reason why Phœnician seamen sought to keep them secret by filling them with horrible portents. Indeed, speaking in general terms, we may say that the great sea struggles, from the dawn of history down to the recent tragedy of the Dardanelles, have raged over those mere threads of water, which dwarf in importance the vast and relatively valueless expanses of water behind them.

The importance of the Hellespont appears from the rise of six successive cities on the hill of Hissarlik or Troy, some three miles inland from its exit into the Ægean. Why should six cities have been built and sacked there? The fact testifies to the enormous value even of early navigation up and down that strait and the Bosporus. But in course of time that hill-site lost its value. Why? The answer to this riddle lies, I believe, in the means of propulsion of early ships. So long as they depended almost entirely on oars, the rowing of even a small craft up some dozen miles of a current, which often runs at five knots,[1] was a severe test for the hardiest crew under the fierce sub-tropical sun. Rest and the replenishment of water supply were a sheer necessity; for in the Hellespont and Bosporus there are few perennial streams, except the Scamander and Simois, which flow past the site of Troy. The city which

---

[1] *Black Sea Pilot*, p. 14.

commanded that water supply could practically control the navigation of the straits.[1] No wonder, then,
that the river gods of the Scamander and Simois
figure prominently in the Trojan War.

But there is another reason arising out of the
feebleness of oar propulsion. After a dozen miles
of rowing against the current, comes the final tussle
at the Narrows; for there the course bends sharply
between the sites of the cities of Sestos and Abydos,
causing baffling eddies. For weary oarsmen to surmount these was so great a strain that shipmen preferred to land their cargoes at or near Assos in the
Gulf of Adramyttium, carry them overland through
the Troad, past the hill of Troy and up the eastern
side of the strait. Above the Narrows they came to
almost still water and could row easily up to the
Propontis. But this alternative route by land also
depended on the good will of the men of the Troad;
and it was natural that all the Phrygians should combine in exacting toll from aliens who used that route;
and equally natural that the latter should combine
in self-defence. These facts caused many struggles
between the landsmen who controlled and the oarsmen who used the Hellespont. They may have been
a contributory cause of the Trojan War; and certainly they increased the rivalries between Greeks
and Phœnicians, so soon as both peoples sought to
gain the trade of the Euxine.

[1] Leaf, W., *Troy: a Study in Homeric Geography*, pp. 252 ff.

We here come to the question—Did the Phœnicians give nautical information to the later comers, the Greeks? Such is the thesis, first suggested by Strabo,[1] and elaborated in that remarkable book of M. Victor Bérard, *Les Phéniciens et l'Odysée*. It is inspired by great learning, winged with a vivid imagination; but I cannot accept its main contention —that the *Odyssey* was largely the fruit of the sea lore of the Phœnicians. For reasons already stated I hold that they tried to keep their knowledge to themselves; and that, if they told them anything about their trade routes, it was with the purpose of scaring them off. Consider the monstrous legends about the Straits of Messina, and the exit from the Euxine guarded by clashing rocks—two crucial straits which the Phœnicians wanted to keep closed. Or think of the terrors of Oceanus, which the ships of Tarshish regularly braved. Another explanation is that these stories came down from the sea lore of the Minoan Age, earlier than the Phœnician.[2]

Moreover, the geography of the *Odyssey* is a most ingenious puzzle, calculated to deceive and exasperate would-be adventurers in the wake of Odysseus. Outside the Ægean Sea and the Straits of Messina no landmark is recognizable; all is vague and

[1] Strabo, III, 150.
[2] An acute suggestion, due to Cary and Warmington, *The Ancient Explorers*, p. 18.

deceptive. From the point of view of geography the
Odyssey is a kind of cross-word puzzle gone mad.
For example, only once is there any indication as
to shaping your course by night—a feat in which
Phœnician seamen were experts and probably the
only experts. This one case is where Calypso bids
Odysseus, when he escaped from her sweet thraldom
at Ogygia, to keep the constellation of the Great
Bear on his left hand—at night of course.[1] Then he
will reach the Phæacian Mountains, whence he may
finally reach Ithaca. But, as geography, all that is a
mere blind; for we begin at Ogygia, which is nowhere, and end at the Phæacian Mountains, which
are left vague. So the one piece of scientific navigation enshrined in the *Odyssey* is due to a bit of
clever fooling.[2]

While I am referring to the poetry of the Mediterranean, may I mention the delightful vignette with
which Matthew Arnold adorned the close of his
Scholar Gipsy? In beautiful imagery he compares the
close of the career of that nervy recluse with that of
the grave Tyrian trader, who, when he saw the
bustling Greek rival heave in sight, recognized that
his day was past and over. Doubtless you remember
the scene—how that coy Phœnician

---

[1] *Odyssey*, v, 272.

[2] The attempt of Mr Gladstone in *Juventus Mundi* to
construct a map of the geography of the *Odyssey* seems to me
a failure.

—saw the merry Grecian coaster come,
Freighted with amber grapes and Chian wine,
Green bursting figs, and tunnies steeped in brine,
And knew the intruders on his ancient home
—The young light-hearted masters of the waves.

Matthew Arnold pictures the Tyrian as at once discerning the doom of his old world, and shaking out more sail to make for far Iberia. Not so the truth, I believe. The hard reality would be prompt manœuvring for a flank position and a deadly blow dealt amidships against that hated rival.

To recur to the Græco-Phœnician rivalries, which were accentuated by the efforts to capture the control of the Hellespont, it is clear that the Greeks, owing to their greater man power and colonizing ability, gained the upper hand, especially after they founded Abydos at the Narrows, and Lampsakos and Parion near by. Further, the settlement of Cyzicus on the isthmus in the Propontis secured Greek supremacy in that sea; and after about 650 B.C., when they occupied the superb site of Byzantium, the best links with the Euxine were in Greek hands; and therefore the valuable sea-borne trade thence in corn, fish and metals must have been controlled by them.

If the Greeks quarrelled among themselves for a share in that valuable commerce, how much more must the Phœnicians have sought to dislodge them all? Finally, Greek disunion presented an opportunity for the Phœnicians to compass their end; and they sought it through the rapidly growing might of Persia. Accepting her supremacy on land, they made themselves necessary at sea to that essentially continental power. As they had been of service before to the Assyrians and Babylonians, so now they became the sea-leaders to the latest of Asiatic conquerors; and the statements of Herodotus and Thucydides prove that only by the fleets and the seacraft of the Phœnicians did Darius succeed, first in subduing the Ionian Greeks, and thereafter in crushing their formidable revolt in the year 499 B.C. The seamen of Tyre and Sidon thus prepared the way for the Persian invasion of Europe. Indeed, it is impossible not to admire the skill with which these persistent seamen now utilized the formidable and conquering might of Persia to root out their Greek rivals both from the coast of Ionia, and then from the key positions on the Bosporus and Hellespont. Never, perhaps, has a race of traders used its military overlords so cleverly for the purpose of reasserting trade supremacy. Thus was set moving that snowball strategy which rolled up nearly all the naval and military forces of the easternmost Greeks on the side of Persia against their motherland. Specially eager were the Phœnicians in expelling the Byzantines and burning neighbouring Greek colonies. They also secured for Darius the island of Thasos where they had formerly discovered and worked a gold mine. His successor, Xerxes, placed a high value on the Phœnician contingent which formed the backbone of the mighty armada that, in 480 B.C., came near to blotting out the existence of Athens.

We must dismiss the wild estimate of Herodotus, that the Great King led more than five and a quarter million men into Greece; for Thrace, Macedonia and Thessaly could not have fed such a host, though its commissariat department was helped by supplies from the fleet, and Herodotus accepts the quaint story that its advance may have been furthered by occasional drinking dry of rivers (and one salt lake!) that barred the way. Very soon, indeed, did legend begin to blur the outlines of the Battle of Salamis; for Æschylus, who may have been one of the seamen in the Athenian contingent, while estimating the total Greek fleet at 310 triremes, reckons that of Xerxes at 1000—an improbable number, unless we include storeships and assign that number to the whole campaign. Æschylus adds that 207 were of special speed. Surely these words do not imply that these 207 were additional ships, but rather that they were the best of the 1000. Herodotus, however, makes the Persian total 1207;[1] and he evidently took the 207 as a separate body. I think he copied Æschylus, and probably copied him wrongly. In any case, the odds were against the Greeks, though

[1] Herodotus, VII, 89.

perhaps not so heavily as their patriotic poet and
historian maintained.

We shall understand both the Persian strategy
before Salamis, and the Greek tactics during the

battle, if we remember what had happened not long
before off Cape Artemisium, which is at the northern
entrance to the long, winding channel inside Eubœa.
Xerxes had there sought to surround the smaller
Greek force in front and to cut off its retreat at the
Narrows, called Euripus, far away in its rear. He

might have succeeded but for the summer storm which destroyed his considerable force sent round Eubœa to block the Euripus from the south.[1] Owing to that storm (an unusual event at that time of the year) his circumventing strategy failed.

Meanwhile, the Greeks, holding the northern or Artemisian entrance to the strait, trusted to the narrowness of the channel to protect their flanks from the overlapping wings of the main Persian force, which, posted farther out, surpassed them both in numbers and speed and could therefore outflank them. Why the defenders should have assumed the offensive is a mystery, especially as their ships were heavier and could deal deadly blows by ramming only from a short distance. They resolved, however, to put all to the test. So, grouping their sterns near together, and turning their prows outward, they advanced fanwise against the hostile formation spread out along the circumference. Thanks to these tactics they gained successes at some points, and after capturing 30 triremes (so Herodotus states),[2] retired to the Artemisian strand. The storm above referred to damaged the enemy out in the open and encouraged the Greeks to sail forth on the morrow and attack, but this time with no advantage, though

[1] Tarn, Dr W. W., in *Journal of Hellenic Studies*, xxviii, 202, discredits the story of this storm. See maps of Artemisium and Salamis on pp. 57 and 60.

[2] Herodotus, viii, 11.

their position level with the strand offered a safe retreat. On the third day the Persian armada assumed
the offensive, only to fall into disorder as it neared
the Greek position, while the defenders, waiting at
the entrance to the strait, now gained some advantage. But Herodotus, while claiming for them the
victory, admits that the Athenians, half of whose
force suffered badly, desired to retreat[1]—an issue
which became inevitable when news arrived of the
disaster to the land force of Leonidas at Thermopylæ. Thanks to the rough handling of the Persian
armada, it did not pursue through the strait, and
eventually the Greeks reassembled off Salamis, while
the Persians followed to the Bay of Phalerum and
their army occupied Athens, beating down also the
forlorn hope which clung to the Acropolis. The last
resource of Athens was in her fleet; but Themistocles
did not, like most of the Greeks, despair; for he had
learnt the lesson of the three days' fighting at Artemisium, that the chief chance of the Greeks was in
narrow waters, like those between the tail (Cynosura) of Salamis and the mainland of Attica; while it
was also a psychological certainty that Xerxes and
his captains would rush on to exterminate the elusive
Greek fleet and end the war. Accordingly, Themistocles urged the Spartans and Corinthians not to
desert the Athenians but to help them in a supreme
effort behind the Cynosura of Salamis; for "our ships

[1] Herodotus, VIII, 15–18.

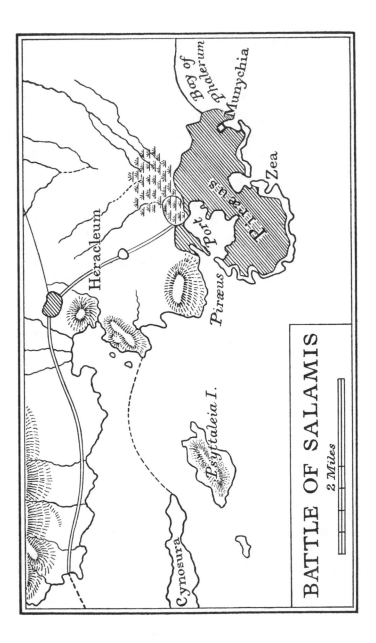

Bay of Phalerum

Munychia

Zea

Piræus

Port Piræus

Heracleum

Cynosura

Psyttaleia I.

BATTLE OF SALAMIS

2 Miles

are heavier and fewer than the enemy's", and "to fight in a narrow space is favourable to us, in the open, to the enemy".[1]

In order to lure the Persian armada into the Salamis Narrows, Themistocles sent a slave to warn Xerxes that the Greeks were about to escape by night from their desperate position. Naturally enough, after the hurried escape of the Greeks from Artemisium, Xerxes believed this story, which coincided with his own expectations of what the beaten and quarrelsome Greeks were likely to do. He therefore despatched a body of ships to block up the western or Megara exit of the Eleusinian Gulf, in the rear of the Greeks, so as to prevent their flight by that channel. As for his main force he ordered it, after nightfall, to row out from the Bay of Phalerum towards the winding eastern entrance to that gulf, and to patrol before it all night in triple lines (ἐν στοίχοις τρισìν).[2] He further landed troops on the Isle of Psyttaleia which lies across part of that entrance. He now considered the Greeks caught in a trap.

In reality the Persian armada was about to run into the Greek trap, which Themistocles had skilfully prepared. For not only did his trick compel even the dissident Spartans and others to fight the

[1] Herodotus, VIII, 62.

[2] Æschylus, *Persae*, l. 368. I take these words to mean in triple lines, not as rendered in *Camb. Ancient Hist.* IV, p. 308.

national enemy, but it led that enemy to patrol the strait all night and expose his crews, weary and breakfastless, to a fight with the Greeks, now well rested and perforce united. Dismay seized on the Persians as they saw the Greek force file out from under the shelter of Salamis and heard the war pæan rising triumphant and echoed by cliff after cliff all round. They had come to hunt down a defeated and divided enemy; they saw him come forth defiant and united.

Moreover their mass must enter the strait either between the "Cynosura" of Salamis and the islet of Psyttaleia or between that islet and the mainland of Attica. The hog's back of the intervening islet hindered all sight of the two parts of the advancing Persian host, and therefore precluded a well-concerted advance. In the narrower channel, west of Psyttaleia, were the Phœnicians (probably 207 triremes), who soon were to meet the Athenians posted on the western side of the defenders' line. In the wider channel (some 1000 yards wide) east of the islet, the main force of Xerxes struggled forward. It was composed largely of Ionian Greeks who, though fighting under compulsion, advanced eagerly under the jealous gaze of Xerxes, who was seated on a spur commanding a view of the scene of action.

Thus Salamis was Artemisium over again, but with these disadvantages superadded for the invaders. Psyttaleia hindered a united Persian onset;

and the presence of Xerxes led to a nervous and probably precipitate advance of the main body into the Narrows; while the Phœnician left wing had to make an awkward left turn as it entered the narrowest part of the strait. No wonder that the Persian attack was confused and "according to no plan";[1] for their triple lines, which had all night patrolled the approaches, now had to move forward (probably in columns abreast) into a funnel which inevitably cramped and disordered their advancing "flood"— as Æschylus terms it.

As for the Greeks, they too were in some confusion. According to Herodotus, they were in doubt whether to rush forward and attack at once, or "to fight backwardly", as Themistocles advised. His advice was certainly followed by the Athenians at the western end; and their novel ruse was carried so far that he even pictures a female form hovering over the Greeks and chiding them with the words "Madmen, how long will ye backwater?" That thought must have agonized thousands of Athenian women thronging the heights of Salamis as they saw their defenders retiring. Their fears were groundless. The Athenian wing, and probably most of the Greek force, were carrying out to the full the retirement into the Narrows which Themistocles, at Artemisium, had seen to be the only safe tactics for the outnumbered and outpaced Greeks. Now, at the

---

[1] Herodotus, VIII, 86.

fitting moment, they charged home into the huddling mass in front, and probably the Athenians crashed with deadly effect into the still wheeling line of the Phœnicians.

No impression of confusion among the defenders appears in the terse and dramatic account of the battle given by the Persian messenger in the drama of Æschylus. And this is but natural; for slight and passing was the indecision among the Greeks compared with the jostlings of the Persian armada as it struggled forward into the strait. This is how he pictures it (I quote Dean Plumptre's translation):

> And first the mighty flood
> Of Persian host held out. But when the ships
> Were crowded in the strait, nor could they give
> Help to each other, they with mutual shocks
> With beaks of bronze went crushing each the other,
> Shivering the rowers' benches. And the ships
> Of Hellas, with manœuvring not unskilful,
> Charged circling round them.[1] And the hulls of ships
> Floated capsized, nor could the sea be seen,
> Strown as it was with wrecks and carcases.
> ....
> And they, as men spear tunnies, or a haul
> Of other fishes, with the shafts of oars
> Or spars of wrecks, went smiting, cleaving down.

This graphic description portrays the Greeks as ranged in a great curve around the Persian force as it became jammed in the strait. In short the victory

[1] The actual words of Æschylus imply that the Greeks were in a circular formation and kept smiting the enemy.

of the Greeks was due to their use of the Narrows
leading to Eleusis Bay; for, under the skilful lead of
Themistocles they adopted the formation likely to
punish the enemy most severely when he pushed into
it. At last, and by guile, the men of the Narrows
beat the skilled long-distance seamen. Or rather,
Xerxes was utterly outwitted by the Greek leader,
the result being that the Persian armada was thrust
into a position where its skill and speed were useless, and where numbers merely added to the awful
débâcle. It is not too much to say that, in the Salamis
campaign, Themistocles pointed the way towards
correct naval strategy and tactics for the weaker
force. He chose most advantageously both the site
for the battle and the method of the defence.

Xerxes, though pretending for a time to be about
to resume the offensive, prepared to make off for
the Hellespont, lest the Greeks break his bridge of
boats at that crucial point and so cut him off from
Asia. In point of fact, a storm had already broken
that bridge; and it was on the relics of his fleet that
he crossed over into Asia. A year or more later his
army followed him thither.

With true insight Herodotus concludes his history
of the Persian War with the scene of the victorious
Athenians bringing back from the Hellespont the
shore cables of the Persian bridge of boats and de-
dicating them to the gods. They and he rightly saw
that the Hellespont was the key to Europe. The

continent was safe so long as that strait was in the hands of the chief naval power of the Greeks. Thus Salamis and its sequel decided that the future of Europe lay with the Greeks, not with Asiatics. Indeed, that triumph proved to be the first of several gained by the Greeks over the Phœnicians, whose sea power was finally to be overthrown by that champion of Hellenic civilization, Alexander the Great.

NOTE ON *ARTEMISIUM* AND *SALAMIS*

After going over the positions of the Battle of Salamis I am convinced that to study them is more important than to dissect the original narratives with regard to questions of numbers and the like.[1] Whether the Persian armada at Salamis numbered 1207, 1000, 800, or even fewer triremes is, I believe, of less import than its position during the patrol of the previous night and the advance to the attack. On these two topics I follow the guidance of that eyewitness of the battle, Æschylus, who wrote the *Persae* less than eight years afterwards; while the far longer narrative of Herodotus, composed about a generation later, obviously consists of a confused growth of memories and legends which he could not harmonize. Æschylus's estimate of 1000 for the Persian total represents a visual impression; but his subsequent words, I think, prove that the Persian ships spent the night before the battle in "watching the exits" from the Bay of Salamis (*Persae*, verse 367), for they kept "sailing

[1] E.g. *Journal of Hellenic Studies* (1908), xxviii.

across" their patrol space (verse 382)[1]. This must have been between the south-west tail of the Isle of Psyttaleia and the nearest points of Salamis and the Piræus headland. Historians, e.g. Grote, who make the Persians on that night enter the Bay of Salamis, render unintelligible the poet's account of the Persian advance next morning, as described in Chapter II. Surely it was the advance into the narrowing space between the Cynosura of Salamis and the opposite headland of Attica to the east-north-east which caused the fatal crowding and opposed a jostling mass to the charge of the Greek semicircle. Reckoning 100 triremes abreast to a mile, the Greek total of 310 would need at least a three miles' front for proper manœuvring; and in crescent formation, two deep, behind that strait, which is $1\frac{1}{2}$ miles broad, they would have ample space for their full striking power.

Herodotus (VIII, 85) states that the Lacedæmonians rejected or neglected the initial advice of Themistocles "to fight backwardly"—a phrase which I take to apply to the middle of the Greek line. The line would then become an irregular crescent. Æschylus says nothing about the back-watering; but his words (verse 418)— "the Greek ships in a circle skilfully kept smiting them" —imply that the Greek line, which early rowed to its station just behind the strait, became a crescent; and that was surely the best formation for letting in the hostile mass and enclosing it between the pincers of the defence.[2] In short, the strategic foresight of Themistocles

[1] So Goodwin, Prof. W. W., in *Harvard Studies in Classical Philology* (1906), XVII.

[2] So too, How, W. W., in *Journal of Hellenic Studies* (1923), XLIII.

in selecting this ideal position was equalled by his guile in inducing Xerxes both to fight there and to compel the dissident part of the Greek force to stay there. Equally skilful was his tactical insight in persuading the Greek centre to back-water and thus form a crescent. Seemingly, he alone had fully understood the lessons taught by the three unsatisfactory fights off Artemisium, viz. how the smaller, slower but stouter built fleet of the Greeks could avoid being outpaced, outflanked, and overpowered by the speed of the invaders. Also he saw that the position behind the Cynosura of Salamis offered the supreme advantage of shelter in a fairly extensive bay where the defenders could outflank and ram *at close quarters* an enemy who pressed in through a narrowing funnel, in which the Persian superiority in numbers would become a disadvantage. Thus, recent efforts by certain critics to minimize their numbers are futile. Besides, Æschylus gained the impression that the Persian advance was that of a flood (ῥεῦμα), a mental picture of their dense columns moving abreast towards the Narrows.

The difficulty of a well-concerted Persian advance was, I believe, greatly increased by the intervening islet of Psyttaleia, the high ridge of which prevented the Persian centre and right wing seeing the movements of their left, or Phœnician, wing on the west. On this last devolved the most perilous task of the assailants, viz. to wheel briskly round the tip of Cynosura so as to meet betimes the flank charge of the Athenians opposed to them. To do so quickly and yet not leave a gap with the Persian centre was, I judge, impossible for a fleet tired by an all-night patrol, and flurried by a too eager advance.

As the Persian attack bristled with difficulties, how came it that in the council held at Phalerum only one of

Xerxes' advisers warned him against it? Queen Artemisia
alone advised him not to incur that risk, but to keep his
fleet intact near his army, either there, or in the forth-
coming march on the Peloponnese. All the others
advised an immediate attack. Why? Probably because at
Phalerum they were too far off to see the trap which
awaited them beyond Psyttaleia; for only on that islet,
or level with it can the strength of the Greek position
be discerned; but also because they knew of the discontent
of Xerxes with the fleet's actions at Artemisium, and
now sought to minister to his ruling passion, vanity.
If the Persian vanguard marching towards Eleusis, or the
Persian garrison landed on Psyttaleia, had sent a warning
as to the Narrows, it came too late or was disregarded.
Clearly the Queen ran some risk by trying to dissuade
him from fighting again;[1] for he himself believed that
the fleet would do better now if it fought under his
gaze. In the resulting battle his presence on the spur of
Mt Aigaleos must have increased the precipitation of the
Persian onset and therefore the magnitude of the disaster.

Thucydides (I, 74) well summed up the opinion of a
later generation of Greeks—"that he (Themistocles)
was chiefly responsible for their fighting in the straits,
which most clearly saved their cause". But is it not
strange that the Greeks, who were pre-eminently
coasters, should have needed the experiences of Artemisium and then the arguments and guile of Themistocles
to force them into adopting strategy and tactics, which
made the most of their admirable coastline?

It is impossible to discuss here the question whether
Xerxes *consciously* adopted the plan of mastering the

---

[1] Herodotus, VIII, 68, 69.

coasts of the Eastern Mediterranean in order to exhaust
the recalcitrant part of the Greeks and starve out their
fleets. Naval strategy was as yet *in embryo*. He came
very near to success, and failed only owing to precipitate
action at Salamis. May not his many successes by land
action have suggested to Alexander in 332 B.C. the
conquest of the Syrian and Egyptian coasts so as to
ensure his communications against fleet action before
he invaded Persia?

CHAPTER III

THE PUNIC-ROMAN STRUGGLE
FOR SICILY

"I regard...the Hannibalic War as a consequence of that about Sicily." Polybius, iii, 32.

Before we proceed to review the rise of Rome to her position of supremacy in the Mediterranean, we may briefly inquire why the Greeks, after their glorious victories over Persia, did not retain for centuries the proud position of supremacy at sea. Their peninsula is better suited than that of Italy for controlling the Eastern Mediterranean. The answer lies in the sphere of character. The Greeks were too clannish ever to combine firmly as a nation. Glorious in the realms of art and thought, they were mere peevish children in the political sphere. Their union even against Persia was fitful; but far worse was their failure to unite betimes against Philip II of Macedon. Their endless chatter and hopeless schisms, their rejection of the much-needed naval reforms urged by their great patriot, Demosthenes, aroused his despair. He chid them for acting just as Philip would have them act,[1] and ascribed all the successes of that King to the swift advances of the Macedonian army and the akilful use of Macedonian bribes.[2]

Nevertheless, I venture to think Demosthenes ill-

[1] Demosthenes, *Fourth Philippic*, 20.
[2] Demosthenes, *De Corona*, 102, 247.

advised when, after the assassination of Philip, he
and other Athenian patriots did not enter whole-
heartedly into the polity of his more generous successor, Alexander. For this brilliant youth, trained
by Aristotle, admired the Greeks and fashioned his
career on the model of Achilles. Now that he held
Thermopylæ, all the north shore of the Ægean,
above all the Hellespont and Byzantium, which controlled "the corn supply of all Greece",[1] he alone
could make Greece strong and prosperous. Greek
liberties having fallen at Chæronea, was it not well
to clasp the proffered hand of the young Macedonian and support his plan of Hellenizing the
Orient? Greece, owing to her endless feuds, needed
the backing of her Macedonian hinterland. But scorn
of the northern barbarians kept her isolated and
weak.[2]

Possibly, if Alexander the Great had enjoyed the
full confidence of Athens, which he ever coveted, he
would have been less tempted to push on, after his
first great victories over the Persians, to seize the
empire of the distant Orient. That exploit he
achieved with bewildering ease, staying his meteoric
career on the Upper Ganges only because his troops

[1] Demosthenes, *De Corona*, 241.
[2] Curtius, at the end of his *History of Greece*, shows very
ably why Athens could not enter into the plans of Philip,
ostensibly for her benefit; but I cannot see that this argument
holds good for Alexander, the pupil of Aristotle.

imperiously called a halt (324 B.C.). As is well known, all his arts failed to reconcile his Macedonian followers to the oriental state which he now assumed; and even before his tragic death at Babylon in 323 B.C., his mighty empire showed signs of cracking in half. "East was East and West was West"; and even Alexander, with all his boundless power and ineffable charm, could not bind them together. Why was this? The underlying reason for the alienation of East and West was, I believe, as follows. The eastern peoples were shut off by deserts from the peoples of the West; and had for ages led a perfectly different life—the life of the desert, the steppe, and the torrid valleys of the Tigris, Oxus, Indus and Ganges.

On the other hand, the West was the land of the sea, i.e. of the Mediterranean basin. Intercourse over its waters had now imparted a certain unity even to Asia Minor and Europe; for no small part of Asia Minor was Greek, or at least Hellenized. Therefore to rule over Macedonia, Greece, Asia Minor, perhaps also Egypt, was quite feasible, their peoples having long had close commercial intercourse, and indeed, Alexander's destruction of Tyre and foundation of Alexandria promised a complete victory for Greek culture and commerce in the Levant. Thereafter the growing trade of the Mediterranean lands was likely to cement them together. Seas unite, while deserts separate. Accordingly,

Alexander could, without grave difficulty, have welded together all the Mediterranean lands in a great empire based on that sea.

It was not to be. The expanding oriental plans of Alexander finally set nature at defiance. From Macedonia and Thrace as base he strove to control immense tracts of Asia wholly sundered from Europe and inhabited by alien peoples. Surely, he should have been content with building up an Empire of the Centre and West—a plan readily practicable when the Samnites still defied the immature power of Rome. For such an Empire he is said to have had keen yearnings. The rumour has been discredited.[1] But was it not natural for him to wish to make Magna Græcia the base for a great Empire of the West? However that may be, the East had her revenge and closed his career at Babylon. If, ten years earlier, he had limited his eastern ambitions to the Upper Euphrates or Tigris, he might have unified the western world around the Mediterranean; and in that case he would assuredly have diffused over it Hellenic culture far more sympathetically than the stolid Roman was to spread it some three centuries later.

After the Greeks had lost their one supreme champion, their political ineptitudes yielded the Empire of the West to a silent people, which could

[1] By Dr Tarn in *Camb. Ancient Hist.* VI, 384.

at least build. For the Romans had this great advantage over the heady Hellenes, that their imagination did not outrun their common sense; neither did excess of criticism palsy action. Moreover, situated as the Romans were in the middle peninsula of the Mediterranean, they were long free from the eastern allurements which have been fatal to the high-flyers of history, from Alexander to Napoleon. Also, unlike them, Rome in her best days never made war on deserts. She was content to limit her enterprises to the practicable and to deal with one enemy at a time. Her progress, skilfully cemented by alliances, enabled her, though a non-maritime State, to beat down successively all Mediterranean rivals, until she made that sea a Roman lake. Her advance had the terrifying effect of the decrees of fate. But in reality her success was due to qualities denied to Tyre, to the Greeks, to Alexander or to Carthage; for she possessed in a high degree foresight that looked beyond immediate gain, patriotism that rose superior to faction, daring curbed by prudence, and indefatigable hardihood. Moreover, by good fortune rather than design, she began her oversea career with the conquest of the strategic centre of the Mediterranean. Sicily, which had been the undoing of the Athenian Empire, was the making of the Roman Empire.

That beautiful island had been coveted in turn by all the Mediterranean powers; and this is but natural; for it is desirable both for its internal resources and for its commanding position. The island contains large fertile plains and valleys, in which corn and the vine flourish. By comparison with Greece it was a veritable granary and vineyard. No wonder, then, that poorer peoples struggled to acquire it. First in historic times the Phœnicians, then their mighty offshoot, Carthage, then Corinth and Athens, there struggled for mastery. Small though Sicily seems to us, it was a great kingdom to those city states. They looked on Sicily much as Englishmen of the age of Chatham looked on our American colonies, as the nursery of a new and greater England. There is a touch of buoyancy in Greek references to Sicily; and there Greek art and architecture gained in vigour, breadth and grandeur.

But, still more was Sicily coveted for its position; for it dominates the narrow waist of the Mediterranean. That island prolongs the mountain system of Italy, and so belongs to Europe; but it also stretches out far towards the north-eastern tip of the Atlas Mountains of North Africa. Less than 100 miles separates Sicily from Cape Bon, and therefore Sicily renders easy the transit between Europe and North Africa. But, besides beckoning the two continents to intercourse, it separates the Mediterranean Sea into two not very unequal halves. At the strait between Sicily and Cape Bon an enterprising maritime people, holding both shores, and maintaining a good navy, is able to hamper the intercourse between the two great parts of that sea. If such a people cannot altogether bar the way, it can at least make safe intercourse between East and West precarious. In fact, a sea power, occupying both Sicily and the North of Africa, will go far towards gaining command of the whole of the Mediterranean. And in ancient times to command that sea was to rule the known world.

It is therefore not surprising that the enterprising Phœnicians very early founded two colonies in North Africa, viz. Utica and Carthage—the latter about 813 B.C. Nor is it surprising that the latter city, which had the better site, throve amazingly and became for long the great sea power of the Mediterranean, far eclipsing Tyre and Sidon, because it possessed what they lacked, a fertile hinterland. What is not so easy to understand is why the Carthaginians, in the time of their thalassocracy, did not expel the Greek race from the whole of Sicily. If they had thoroughly conquered Sicily, Rome would probably never have gained a foothold there, and would have remained merely a great land power.

It was not enough to hold the west of Sicily, as they did. They must also hold the north-east; for the Strait of Messina is another key point. Remember that the ancient Greeks, especially those of Corinth, Phocis, Corcyra and the neighbouring coasts, used, when possible, to avoid the long stretch of open sea between them and Sicily. As a rule, they preferred to take a coastal route, viz. by Corcyra across the mouth of the Adriatic to the heel of Italy and thence towards the toe. Sometimes their commerce was carried overland from Sybaris to a port on the Tyrrhenian Sea. But their war fleets could not take this cut overland towards Neapolis and Massilia. War fleets must go through the Strait of Messina; and there the power that had a fleet ready would have a great advantage over a fleet whose rowers were probably tired by many days' rowing. Therefore Messina was a point of outstanding strategic importance to a power that sought to control the waist of the Mediterranean.

Yet, in what we may call the Græco-Phœnician age, the Carthaginians never seem to have put forth any persistent efforts to seize and hold that strategic point. Though, after a time of inaction, they made good the defeat which Syracuse dealt them at Himera in 480 B.C., and, a century later captured Messina, yet the Greeks before long recovered that place. In the later wars between Carthage and Syracuse, the Punic forces on the whole tended to prevail; for, as Mommsen points out, during the period 394–278 B.C., Syracuse beat them back only when she had great leaders like Dionysius the Elder, Timoleon, Agathocles, and Pyrrhus; but in the intervals the Carthaginians four times spread eastwards again, and acquired nearly all Sicily, only to be baffled by the great fortress reared by Dionysius on the hill north-west of Syracuse.[1] Those who have seen his mighty fortress (albeit in ruins) of Fort Euryalus will understand why it resisted the repeated attacks of Carthage. Further, the landlocked harbour of Syracuse probably baffled the Carthaginian fleet, as it had first baffled, and then entrapped, the Athenian fleet in 413 B.C.; also the shipwrights of Dionysius invented quadreremes and quinqueremes, which carried the day until Carthage also built them. Thus, it was probably the tough resistance of Syracuse which repeatedly held up the Carthaginian forces in Sicily; and, as the walls and harbour of Syracuse were perforce their chief objective, Messina did not feel their chief weight. That, at least, seems to me a plausible explanation why Messina figures little in the Græco-Punic wars; and I think the Carthaginians erred in not making it betimes their chief stronghold; for its sickle-shaped promontory formed a natural harbour, not indeed equal to that of Syracuse, but by far the best in the strait; and to command that strait was to hold fast the key to North-east Sicily and one of the passages into the West Mediterranean.

We need glance only very briefly at the effort of Pyrrhus to expel the Carthaginians from Sicily. The brave but erratic King of Epirus had dealt a sharp blow to Roman expansion in South Italy,[2] but, tiring

[1] Mommsen, *Hist. of Rome* (Eng. edit. II, 14).
[2] See Homo, L., *Primitive Italy and the Beginnings of Roman Imperialism*, ch. 4.

of his efforts, he was about to go to Sicily to help
Syracuse against the Carthaginians, who were then
almost on the point of conquering that great bulwark
of Greek power. The Carthaginians, hearing of his
plan, actually sent their admiral, Mago, to Rome to
frame an alliance[1] (279 B.C.). Their aim was to fan
the embers of the Roman war with Pyrrhus so as to
detain him in Italy and thus leave them free to crush
Syracuse. In this they failed. Pyrrhus went to
Sicily and was proclaimed King of Sicily by the grate-
ful Syracusans. He drove back the Carthaginians to
the west end of the island and even stormed Mt
Erkte, which commands Panormus; so that the Carthaginians soon had only Lilybæum left—a strange
proof of their weakness. Their collapse at that time
is unaccountable, but may be regarded as one of the
many signs of the swift alternations between strength
and weakness, which are characteristic of Semitic
peoples, above all, of mercantile oligarchies.

As usual between Greeks, the victors began to
quarrel; and in a rage Pyrrhus left for Italy (spring
of 275), losing half of his fleet to the Carthaginians
in the transit. This crowned *condottiere* of the ancient
world generally ended by compromising his allies;
and it was so with Tarentum and other Greek
cities of South Italy, for he next left them in the
lurch. Rome now put forth all her strength to sub-
jugate these cities, and she conquered them, from

[1] Polybius, III, 25.

Tarentum in 272 to Rhegium in 270. She treated them with politic clemency. Each city became a *socius navalis,* and doubtless helped Rome greatly in the naval wars of the near future.[1] For Rome finally prevailed, not merely by the persistence with which she fought out her wars, but also by the clemency with which she often treated her enemies in the hour of triumph. "Parcere subjectis, et debellare superbos" was frequently her motto.

She now, after 270 B.C., faced the welter of Sicily. At this time, by great good fortune, Messina invited the Romans to cross over and help her against Hiero II, King of Syracuse, who was about to capture it. The people of Messina were then in sore straits. During some 18 years they had been under the yoke of a band of Campanian mercenaries, who had seized the city, killed the men and possessed themselves of their womenfolk, children, and property. These mercenary brigands called themselves Mamertines ("Men of Mars"); and their hand was against every man. Carthage had helped them so as to foil, first Pyrrhus, and, later, Hiero when he marched north to subdue them. But Hiero besieged them long and reduced them to such a condition of famine that they now resolved to call in the aid of Rome. Those scoundrelly Mamertines little knew that their invitation was destined to launch Rome on a career of oversea conquest.

[1] Ihne, *Hist. of Rome* (Eng. ed. IV, 112–14).

To come to the aid of a band of fierce mutineers
and pirates like the Mamertines aroused the scruples
of the Roman Senate; and it came to no decision. The
question was then referred to the burgesses of Rome,
and they voted for taking the Mamertines into the
Italian confederacy, on the ground that they were
Italians. Of course what the Roman populace wanted
was, not to protect those cut-throats, but to get hold
of Messina. Yet much can be said for their decision;
for at this time Carthage was mistress of the Tyrrhene Sea;[1] and the Carthaginians were in the habit of
capturing every strange ship which sailed towards
Sardinia (then in their power) or towards the Straits
of Gades; and they also threw the crews overboard.
So affirms Eratosthenes, the father of geography.
And, now that Rome had Rhegium as a *socius navalis*,
she would naturally detest having the Carthaginians
as neighbours across the straits. As it was a question
of Messina becoming Roman or virtually Carthaginian, the Roman populace naturally did not hesitate.
It voted for alliance with Messina.

By this momentous vote Rome laid the foundations
of her overseas Empire; for to get a foothold in
anarchic Sicily was like our East India Company
getting a foothold at Surat in the troublous India of
the time after Akbar. The intruder could not, in the
nature of things, stand still. Either he or anarchy

[1] Homo, p. 211. She had overcome in turn the Massilian,
Etruscan and Syracusan fleets.

must prevail; and in the interests of order and civilization we may rejoice that the Roman people took this bold though very irregular step. It was the work of the populace rather than of the governing class; and we may say that the populace stumbled into the track which led on to World Empire.

The Roman force now sent across the strait disregarded the protests made by the Carthaginian admiral and entered Messina. By so doing, Rome mortally offended her ally, Carthage; for the Romans had forcibly entered waters which Carthage held as a *mare clausum*; they had also entered Messina, and even seized the Carthaginian general, Hanno, who very weakly ordered his troops to evacuate the city. For this cowardice Carthage beheaded him and sent a force to rescue that strategic point. Hiero also helped the new Carthaginian force; but another and larger Roman army under Appius Claudius now succeeded in crossing from Rhegium on a dark night; and it soon routed both the Carthaginians and Hiero. Next year Rome pursued her triumphs in Sicily over those somewhat discordant allies and beat them soundly. Hiero and the Syracusans had learnt their lesson, and now made peace with Rome, a peace which they loyally observed to the end of Hiero's career. By his help in granting supplies the Romans were firmly established in Sicily; and in the year 262 won a great victory outside Agrigentum which drove the Carthaginians back to their western strongholds, where their fleet could more easily help in the defence.

Nothing in this first crucial phase of the First Punic War is so surprising as the passivity of the Carthaginian fleet. Surely it is a sign of singular slackness that a great maritime people like the Carthaginians should have made so poor a defence at sea against a people who were mere tyros on that element. We very rarely hear of any Roman warships before 281 B.C. when ten of them appeared off Tarentum and were promptly destroyed by the insulted Tarentines. Yet in less than twenty years Rome was able to send large forces across the Strait of Messina, and not once were they destroyed *en route*. Now, it was not very difficult to evade an enemy at night, or trick him as to the real place of crossing (as Garibaldi tricked the Bourbon ships there in 1860); but to miss the enemy several times over bespeaks strange slackness on the part of the best sailors of the ancient world. I give up the riddle as inexplicable;[1] but the fact may be regarded as a sign of the frequent weakness of the Carthaginians and their lack of foresight at great crises. If they wished to maintain their rigid and cruel monopoly over the

[1] Polybius (I, 19, 20) scarcely notes their inactivity. It is strange that, though he travelled much by sea, yet he scarcely noticed naval affairs. His lost work on *Tactics* was probably devoted almost entirely to military affairs (*Camb. Ancient Hist.* VIII, 6).

West Mediterranean, they should have sent every available ship to East Sicily to destroy the scratch collections of local craft first used by the Romans; for the Romans, though formidable on land, were as yet without war-experience at sea. The doom of Carthage was fixed largely by the stupid lethargy of her navy in the crucial years when the Romans first ventured across the Straits of Messina.

Now, when the Romans had seized, or shall we say filched, the key of the Mediterranean, they found the difficulty of keeping it; for Carthage, at last stung to action, pursued guerrilla tactics at sea with annoying success. She devastated, or levied ransom, from many Sicilian and Italian towns. But such tactics in the long run tend to be destructive of the State which employs them; for they exasperate but do not annihilate; and a self-respecting people will strain every nerve to defeat them. In short, the guerrilla tactics of Carthage at sea perforce made the Romans a maritime people. Nothing in their history struck Polybius more than their determination; for (says he) "they had never given a thought to the sea". Yet now they took the matter in hand boldly and attacked those who had long held undisputed command of the sea.[1]

The raids of the Carthaginians also tended to bind the Greeks of Magna Græcia to the Roman cause. Several were already her *socii navales*; and they and

[1] Polybius, i, 20.

others must have helped her greatly. It is therefore by no means incredible that Rome launched a fleet of 100 quinqueremes and 20 triremes within a year (260 B.C.). They were built on the model of a Carthaginian warship which had been wrecked; and rowing was practised first on land.

What was remarkable in the Roman effort was the invention of the *corvus*.[1] This was a light but fairly long bridge, fastened swivel-fashion at the bow, which could be lowered quickly on the enemy's deck which it gripped by a sharp iron spike. This bridge, or gangway (*corvus*) could fall either forwards or on either side. Apparently this skilful invention decided the issue of the first decisive battle which was fought off Mylæ, to the north-west of Messina (260 B.C.). There the Carthaginians advanced with 130 sail against the slower and cumbrous-looking Roman fleet. But they were astonished at what happened. As they charged forward, the *corvi* fell on them and held them fast. Roman legionaries rushed on board and carried the ships with ease; for, as a rule, the Carthaginians used few soldiers afloat; and the Romans had crowded their craft with well-armed legionaries. So (as Polybius says) the battle became like a land battle; for when the hinder Punic ranks retired so as to execute the deadly charge in flank, round swung the *corvi* and gripped them by a sideways fall. No greater

[1] See note on the *corvus* at the end of this chapter.

surprise has ever occurred at sea. About 50 Carthaginian ships were captured or sunk, including that of their admiral, Hannibal. No Roman ship seems to have been lost; and this terrible blow went far towards demoralizing the beaten enemy. It also enabled the Romans to gain successes *in* Sicily.

The blow was so overwhelming that perhaps the Romans might have struck with success at Carthage herself. For that reckless adventurer, Agathocles, when at the nadir of his fortunes in Sicily, just 50 years earlier, had dared to leave his city, Syracuse, besieged in order to deal a home thrust at Carthage herself, and had nearly succeeded with only 60 ships (which he burnt to render his men desperate). Therefore what might not the victorious Roman fleet now effect? The Carthaginians were generally at feud among themselves, and still more often were daunted by a heavy blow. So why not dare all, as Agathocles had done, and with all but complete success? For some unknown reason, the Romans were prudent. Perhaps they could not face the long voyage over unknown waters. At any rate, they turned to a nearer sphere, Corsica, and burnt some of the Carthaginian posts there, but really effected nothing lasting. Finally, in 256 B.C. (i.e. four years after Mylæ), the Senate resolved to strike at Carthage—a decision equally bold and correct.

Now was seen the value of Sicily. The great Roman fleet of 330 vessels mustered first at Messina;

and, later, on the south coast of Sicily it took on board four legions under the consuls, Regulus and Volso. This mighty force encountered as many as 350 Carthaginian vessels off Ecnomus. In the ensuing battle the Carthaginians failed both in tactics and in grit, for, when the Roman centre was thrown far forward against the enemy's centre which withdrew somewhat, the Punic wings were not used effectively to charge it on both flanks and in rear; but (so says Polybius) one wing made off for the Roman divisions (partly horse-transports and therefore slow) which had been left behind. Consequently the Roman centre was not crushed and finally beat off the unskilful and ill-pressed attack. Probably in all parts of this confused *mêlée* the boarding rush of trained legionaries over the *corvi* proved to be the decisive factor. In the end the Romans lost 24 vessels sunk; but they captured 64, and sank more than 30.[1]

This victory enabled them to land their 40,000 troops in Africa, and they left the fleet protected by an entrenched naval camp—a fact that shows that they could quickly beach and haul up their vessels, which therefore must have been comparatively light. Their troops advanced quickly towards Carthage;

[1] Polybius (i, 26–8). He says that each Roman ship had 300 rowers and 120 soldiers or, in all, 140,000 men. He thinks the Carthaginians had on board 150,000 men. Probably they included more soldiers than usual. For a conjectural plan see Shepard, A. M., *Sea Power in Ancient History*, p. 150.

and, as happened at the time of Agathocles's invasion, the towns subject to Carthage for the most part revolted, while the warlike Numidians also helped the Roman invaders, who therefore gained several successes. Nevertheless, as the Roman Senate demanded impossible terms (especially that Carthage should give up her fleet and furnish vessels to help Rome in her wars), the Carthaginians resolved to struggle on.

Their courage was rewarded. Hamilcar soon brought a welcome reinforcement of trained troops from West Sicily, which had evaded the Roman watch. The desperate efforts of the Carthaginians, now led by the Spartan, Xanthippus, had their reward in a complete defeat of the over-confident Romans, who, in a state of panic, sought refuge at their camp at Clupea. The Senate at Rome (also in a panic) soon despatched a large fleet to rescue the beaten force. It gained a victory over Carthaginian ships which sought to stay it off the Hermæan Cape (now Cape Bon); and, sailing on, it rescued the scanty relics of the army of Regulus.

The return voyage was disastrous. Beset by the Roman defect of obstinacy, a quality highly serviceable against men, but fatal against nature, the Roman admirals gave an order, against the advice of the pilots, to sail northwards in doubtful weather. Soon after, even in the month of July, off Camarina on the exposed south coast of Sicily, a terrible storm broke on the fleet, and 284 Roman ships foundered with all on board, i.e. with the loss of nearly 120,000 men.[1] Undismayed, the Roman Senate forthwith ordered 220 ships to be built; and they were ready for sea in three months.

The Carthaginian Senate, however, also made great efforts and sent to Sicily a considerable force, which was especially strong in elephants; for as many as 140 were now sent over. How the Carthaginians managed to induce 140 elephants to go on board ship, and, still more, to remain quiet on the ships during a voyage of 100 miles, baffles the imagination. They must have constructed some elephant transports, in which the beasts were held fast; and probably the transports were either sailing craft or were towed by rowing tugs. However it was accomplished, the feat was among the most marvellous ever accomplished by man. But even 140 elephants could not make up for the poorness of the Carthaginian infantry. Finally, in 254 B.C., the new Roman fleet and its army succeeded in taking Panormus, which, along with its mountain bastion of Ercte, had formed the chief Punic stronghold in Sicily. It now became the chief stronghold of the Romans, and its capture led to the reduction of other towns in the north and west.

But once more the Roman admirals threw away a fleet. Against the advice of the sea captains they

[1] Polybius, I, 37.

ordered the fleet, at the end of the campaign, to sail direct from Panormus to the mouth of the Tiber. In that long stretch of open sea a storm burst on them which sank more than 150 ships, with some 60,000 men.[1] This terrible loss daunted for a time the spirits of the Romans, and made them more than ever hate the sea. Thenceforth the Senate resolved to maintain only a small fleet of 60 vessels and to pursue what may be termed privateering tactics.

This false strategy sacrificed the great aim (the winning of the war at the essential point, Carthage) to the winning of prizes here and there. And its bad results were accentuated by two serious mishaps at sea. The Roman Consul, Publius Claudius, sought to surprise and cut off the Carthaginian fleet in the harbour of Drepanum, but was skilfully outmanœuvred by the defenders and badly defeated. This, the only considerable victory at sea of the Carthaginians, was due mainly to their skill and speed.[2] The other consul also fared as badly off Lilybæum, losing most of the Roman transports in a battle, and in a storm which came on afterwards. Thus the Romans lost by storms nearly the whole of four great fleets with armies on board, while an army had been almost destroyed near Carthage. The war therefore languished; for indeed both sides were exhausted by the strain, and neither could then make the supreme effort which wins the war over a half demoralized foe.

[1] 253 B.C. Polybius, I, 39.   [3] *Ibid.* I, 51.

Consequently the war lingered on during six uneventful years. Towards the close of that time Hamilcar (Barca) occupied Mt Ercte and threatened Panormus. Had the Carthaginian Senate supported him effectively he might perhaps have reconquered West Sicily for the Phœnicians. But that hide-bound body did not support him.

Victory finally inclined to the side which showed most patriotism and untiring persistence. And it is noteworthy that, though the Roman Senate clung to its privateering methods, yet the Roman people now at last resolved on bolder and more effective strategy: for it resolved by private subscriptions to build one more fleet. Splendidly the money came in, even in the twenty-second year of a very costly war; and some 200 quinqueremes were presented to the State. They were built on the model of the "Rhodian" ship, a fast blockade-runner.[1] Carthage made no corresponding effort; and the new Roman fleet won the decisive battle of the war off the Isle of Ægusa, where by good discipline and superior tactics it annihilated the weaker Carthaginian fleet, heavily loaded and cumbered by many transports. It sank 50 ships and captured 70.[2]

This victory at sea placed Sicily in their hands; and the treaty of a few weeks later ceded the last Punic

[1] Polybius, I, 47, 59. A sign that the Romans now trusted mainly to speed.
[2] *Ibid.* I, 60.

posts in that island to Rome (241 B.C.). Moreover, the victor claimed a ransom for the enemy forces which she allowed to evacuate Sicily. In this ignominious way the Phœnicians lost the most important island of the Mediterranean, large parts of which they had held for 400 years. Thus ended the war of 24 years for Sicily—"the longest, most continuous and greatest war we know of".[1]

To allow the Carthaginian troops to go home for ransom to a half bankrupt capital was a masterpiece of cunning; for nearly all were mercenaries; and, as Carthage could not, or would not, pay them, the army, when reunited near Carthage, mutinied; and only the genius of Hamilcar (Barca) averted the utter ruin of the State. As a natural sequel to this mutiny, Carthaginian garrisons in Sardinia also rebelled and offered to place their posts in the hands of the Romans, who thus stepped in easily and ("contrary to all justice", says Polybius) secured the chief towns on the coast. They acquired those of Corsica soon after. Thus in the years following the war Sardinia and Corsica fell to Rome, which therefore had to become a great naval power in order to hold these dominating positions. And, as her organization was solid, and her will firm, she did hold them. Consequently, the civilization of the Western

[1] Polybius, i, 63. The Romans lost about 700 quinqueremes, i.e. close on 300,000 men. The Carthaginians 500, i.e. about 220,000 men.

Mediterranean was destined to be a Roman civilization, finally tinged with Greek culture; not a Punic civilization, utterly alien to Greek culture.

Note finally that not even the wonderful genius of Hannibal (son of Hamilcar Barca) could reverse the results of this First Punic War. By the time of the Second Punic War Rome had a firm hold on Sicily, and, even in her critical time after Cannæ, when Syracuse revolted against her, that hold was not withdrawn. But it is noteworthy that a Carthaginian army of 25,000 men, under Himilco, was landed in the south of Sicily, and gained several successes (213 B.C.). What, then, might not have been effected by Hannibal, if, five years before, with his larger force and supreme genius he had been able to strike at Rome through Sicily! I say, if he had been able; but he was not able owing to Rome's mastery of the sea.[1]

Nevertheless, it is worth while reckoning up the advantages which would have been his if he had had a chance of gaining such mastery, and had held West Sicily. From Panormus he could have crossed into Italy with little difficulty; and if we accept as correct Polybius's estimate of 90,000 foot, 12,000 horse and 37 elephants as his initial strength at New Carthage, so great a force landing on the toe of Italy would have menaced Rome with almost certain disaster.

[1] *Camb. Ancient Hist.* VIII, 35.

Acting from Sicily (not Spain) as base, he would not
have suffered the losses in men and horses[1] which so
terribly weakened him in Gaul and in the passage of
the Alps. As it was, he probably had after the passage
of the Alps only 20,000 foot and 6000 horse;[2] but
apparently all his elephants survived though (says
Polybius) "in a wretched condition from hunger",
and many of their mahouts had been drowned in the
Rhone.[3] Thus, during his march of some 800 or 900
miles from South-east Spain into North Italy he had
lost nearly three-fourths of his army before he came
to grips with the Romans on the Ticino, while the
survivors were "more like beasts than men owing
to their hardships".[4] His chief advantage in the
Alpine route was the support by the warlike Gauls
of North-west Italy. But did that support make up
for the terrible losses in his African and Iberian
troops? Probably Hannibal over-estimated the value
of Gallic help as much as he under-estimated the
difficulty of the land march.

On the other hand, if he could have operated
through Sicily, would he not have gained considerable help from the disaffected Greeks of Magna
Græcia? There was great discontent there, which

[1] Polybius, III, 33–46, 55.

[2] *Ibid.* III, 56: Livy, XXI, 38, gives this as the lowest
estimate.

[3] Seemingly the elephants recovered by the time of the
fight on the Trebia (Dec.): for they were formidable there
(Polybius, III, 74). [4] *Ibid.* III, 60.

would have blazed forth if Carthage had had enough energy to support him with a great fleet, able to render incalculable aid during his march along the coast northwards towards Lucania. What the support of a fleet meant to a great army Xerxes's mighty effort had shown. That support was now denied to Hannibal, who received miserably small help from the Carthaginian navy.[1]

Another result of Rome's supremacy at sea was that it enabled her to attack Hannibal's base in Spain and compelled him to draw thence his reinforcements by the long and dangerous march over the Alps; and they availed little when he was shut up in the south of Italy. For now, like a *retiarius* matched against an invincible swordsman, Rome flung her sea-net around him and exposed him to a war of exhaustion not only in Italy itself but in his distant base, Spain. During the nine years after Cannæ the game went on. The great gladiator could retaliate with no effective thrust, while the Roman net and trident overawed nearly all the restive Greeks of South Italy. The hero, therefore, was more and more hemmed in the southern fastnesses; and, for want of a succouring fleet, saw the Greeks terrorized, Macedonian help kept at a distance,[2] and the last brave

[1] For its operations see Livy, xxi, 49–51; xxii, 11, 19–20, 25, 26.

[2] *Camb. Ancient Hist.* viii, 117 ff. See also Huvelin, *La deuxième guerre punique*, ch. 19.

effort at rescue, that of Hasdrubal from Spain, crushed in North Italy. Clearly the underlying cause of Hannibal's glorious failure was the loss of Sicily and of maritime supremacy by Carthage in the First Punic War.

There exists no more tragic figure in military history than Hannibal as he grandly stood at bay in the fastnesses of South Italy, looking for a fleet from Carthage. It never came until too late. Finally Rome, mistress of the sea, struck from Sicily at Carthage herself. Then the Carthaginians bestirred themselves and sent a fleet to bring back Hannibal and his army—again too late even for Hannibal to avert the doom which awaited a decadent people that had lost its grip on the trident.

NOTE ON THE *CORVUS*

This invention was not entirely new; for Herodotus (ix, 98) states that the Greeks before the Battle of Mycale prepared boarding-bridges (ἀποβάθραι) for the sea-fight. Polybius overlooked that fact when he stated (i, 22) that someone suggested the κόραξ (*corvus*). It was, however, an improvement on the ἀποβάθρα in that it had an iron spike at the end, which after the fall fastened the gangway to the enemy's deck. Polybius describes it minutely as having the inner part (12 ft.) horizontal, while the outer part (24 ft.) was kept vertical close to the side of the pole or mast, and could be let fall either forward or sideways.

I cannot accept the assertion of Dr Tarn (*Hellenistic Military and Naval Developments*, p. 149) that the *corvus* is a mere myth because its fall would have upset any ship using it, and that the Romans merely used grapnels. Certainly if the *corvus* fell into the sea, it would be likely to upset its ship; but, if effectively used, its grappling the other ship would steady both. Dr Tarn's objection would apply rather to the ἀποβάθρα, which did not grapple. Besides, heavy armed soldiers unused to the sea would not readily board an enemy ship over grapnels; and, at best, they could only jump over singly, and not with the decisive rush which a fixed gangway would enable them to make.

Another objection is that the *corvus* is not afterwards referred to. But Polybius lays stress on its importance at the Battle of Ecnomus. Indeed the action of the Romans there, in charging with two leading divisions into the midst of the overlapping Carthaginian array, is inconceivable if they had not known the extreme reluctance of the enemy to close; also their rear, encumbered by horse transports must have been overpowered but for the enemy's fear of the *corvi*.

The *corvus*, however, may have been finally superseded as being incompatible with great speed, the value of which had appeared in the exploits of the enemy's "Rhodian", a swift blockade-runner at Lilybæum (Polybius, 1, 46–8; 59). It was on her model that the Romans built their new patriotic fleet of 242 B.C., and I think it likely that then the *corvus* was dropped. Dealings with the Illyrian pirates probably confirmed the preference for high speed, which was clinched by contact with Rhodian fleets.

CHAPTER IV

ROMAN SUPREMACY IN THE WESTERN MEDITERRANEAN

That Greek hostage, Polybius, who perforce spent sixteen years in Rome in the heyday of her world expansion, remarked, with his usual insight, that her amazing rise was due, not to Fortune, but was conformable to reason. For "by schooling themselves in such vast and perilous enterprises they not only gained the courage to aim at universal dominion, but executed their purpose".[1]

It is perhaps doubtful whether the Romans, during their most crucial wars, those with Carthage and Macedon, aimed with set purpose at universal dominion. There are not wanting signs which show their aims to have changed and their maritime policy (the soul of the enterprise) to have wavered in a manner inconsistent with any such purpose. In these brief chapters I cannot examine fully the difficult and elusive subject of motive—elusive even to the cautious, delusive ever to the over confident, inquirer. But I will try to set forth the salient facts which throw light on this question.

First, I suggest that there are two alternative explanations of the rapid rise of the power of Rome. Instead of being due to Fortune or to fixed design, may it not have resulted in her good sense both in acquiring the best maritime allies procurable and

[1] Polybius, I, 63.

also from her skill in wielding superior sea power from the vantage point of the central position? The question just posed, as to Fortune or ambition, has generally been considered, as an abstract proposition and therefore *in vacuo*. It has also been approached from the standpoint of the land. I purpose to approach it from the standpoint of the sea and the navy; also to consider later whether the expansion of Roman power over the Eastern Mediterranean was not due to a series of provocations from that quarter. We shall also see that the challengers in the East proved to be as weak in action as they had been provocative in attitude. In fact that world presented a scene of chaos in which anyone who intervened was half tempted, half compelled, to impose some degree of order; failing which, the resulting disorders on land were certain to breed an ever-increasing brood of robbers at sea. Moreover, the very success of her rule in the West, at which we are now to glance, precluded all thought of allowing widespread anarchy in the East to foster anew that age-long curse of the Mediterranean, piracy. From the time of the Minos to that of the Cæsars the champion of order and commerce had to spread his power wide if only in order to gain security at sea.

Now, to gain a reasonably safe frontier on land is a difficult task which has led to many so-called defensive wars; but to attain security for sea-borne commerce is far more difficult. Nevertheless, as the sequel will show, Rome grappled with both tasks at once. The threats of border tribes like the Gauls pushed her on to the north-west, while the real or supposed threats, first from Carthage, then from the Illyrian pirates, Macedon, Syria and Pontus led her on successively southwards and eastwards. Note the result. Each extension brought increased maritime trade; and every increase of trade compelled her to cope with forces of disorder further and further off. In this process of maritime expansion there was no finality. At last she possessed the whole of the Mediterranean shores, only to discover that order on the frontier still eluded her; and ultimately she found some degree of stability only on the verge of the deserts or trackless forests beyond.

Such is an alternative explanation of the rapid rise of Roman power. Ambition, lust of gold, or of world dominion, doubtless enter into the story.[1] But they are apt to be magnified by those who live too near to the events to see them in their age-long significance. Mediocre minds never see the events for the men. Polybius was feeling his way towards a truer explanation of Rome's meteoric rise: but even he could not view it in the light of centuries. That view is vouchsafed to us; and I think that even the following brief survey will enable us to see how unconscious at all times, and sometimes how casual, was the expansion of this "imperial" people.

[1] See Montesquieu, *Grandeur et Décadence des Romains*, ch. 6.

The one phase of Rome's expansion which bears all the signs of fixed resolve is her long struggle with Carthage. The First Punic War was begun and carried to the end by the will of the people; and their awful losses in men at sea, heavier than those of any other naval war, partly excuse the extremely harsh treatment of the conquered. Rome won Sicily in fair fight; but she then filched from the prostrate foe Sardinia, Corsica and Elba. These gains alone made her mistress of the West Mediterranean; for with the timber of Sicily, Sardinia and Corsica in her hands, not to speak of the iron of Elba, she crippled both commerce and naval construction at Carthage. Not even the genius of Hamilcar and Hannibal could reverse these blows; and, as we have seen, Rome's mastery at sea sufficed to overawe the cities of Magna Græcia and to coop up Hannibal in Calabria, while she built in Sicily the fleet which enabled her to lay Carthage low at Zama.

Thereafter the great Phœnician city existed on sufferance; and when its commerce began to revive, the jealous tirades of old Cato, driven home by the memories of Cannæ, led to that series of humiliating demands which culminated in the sentence of death, that the Carthaginians should destroy their own city and rebuild it ten miles inland—a sign that Rome was resolved to be absolute mistress of the West Mediterranean (146 B.C.).

Then at last the old Punic spirit flared up. Though

a Roman army had landed near by and had been welcomed by the men of Utica, though Carthage was void of ships, void of catapults for the walls, or of elephants in the long lines of empty stalls, yet the untrained almost unarmed citizens long held out against the Roman army, nay, beat it back for a time, until another Scipio (Æmilianus) finally carried the place by storm. Street by street, house by house, thus fell Carthage.

In certain respects her fall is to be regretted. There was enough room for two great cities to share the commerce of the western world, especially as Carthage had specialized in the penetration of Libya and the exploration of the Atlantic coasts. These two spheres meant little or nothing to the Romans, and they now did little towards promoting either the exploration of the interior of Libya or the tracing of its coasts towards the tropics. In these matters they were far less enterprising than the Carthaginians whom they hounded down to ruin. They excelled Carthage immensely in war; for to it they brought gifts of organization in which only two or three Carthaginians equalled them. But in commerce and navigation they fell far below their Punic enemy.

Hence I cannot echo the chorus of ecstatic praise at their triumph. We may grant that the Romans were nearer akin to the Greeks and did much to hand on the Greek spirit. Yet on the other hand Carthage could have handed on the Semitic spirit to a later age; and mankind would have benefited more by the rivalry of the Roman and Semitic civilizations than by the complete triumph of the Roman; for this last tended in the long run to produce sameness and monotony in the western world.

Finally, Rome herself was demoralized by the completeness of her triumph. She would have benefited by competition, even by opposition; and the seeds of her final decay were sown in the decades of military glory which disposed of all rivals and led on her sons to orgies of coarse luxury. The systematic plunder of provincials showed the mental intoxication of her governing class. In three years (so Cicero averred) the exactions of Verres reduced the number of farmers in Sicily from 773 to 318; and these were not little farmers, but landholders and probably Roman burgesses.

Nevertheless, there is one aspect of the Roman triumph which is satisfactory; for it benefited civilization at large. I refer to the fact that, on the whole, the Romans tended to carry on Greek civilization and culture. Here we may well turn aside to trace briefly the influence of the Græco-Roman union on the life of Gaul. This is best seen in the history of Marseilles. That town is in many ways the mother-city of Western Europe. She has exerted a far-reaching influence on Gaul and therefore on France. She was a centre of trade and culture in days when Paris (Lutetia Parisiorum) was a small town of mud huts on an island in the Seine. During hundreds of years before Paris existed Massilia was sending the products of the East up the Rhone Valley and received down it stores of amber, tin and corn which she forwarded first of all to Greece, then to the devouring vortex of Rome.

Let us therefore take note of Massilia; for she is certainly the mother city of Southern Gaul. A battle royal rages as to her origin. It has been ascribed to a Phœnician source on the ground that the Phœnicians, coasting along the Ligurian shores, would certainly be attracted by the islets off Massilia and by the cove and two promontories, which form a natural harbour near the mouth of the Rhone. Also, the champions of a Phœnician origin point out that Punic medals and tokens have been found there.[1] Champions of a purely Greek origin of Massilia argue that her old harbour is landlocked, and that the suspicious Phœnicians never shut themselves up in such harbours, for fear of being trapped by the natives. As for the Punic objects found there, they may belong to a later Carthaginian occupation of the post.[2] It is admitted, however, that the Phœnicians certainly held other posts on that coast, viz. Pyrene (at the east end of the Pyrenees), at Caccabarias near the mouth of the Rhone, at Portus Melkarthis (Villa-

[1] Desjardins, M. E., *Géographie de la Gaule romaine*, ii, 136 ff.

[2] Castanier, P., *La Provence pré-historique* (Paris, 1893).

franca) and Herakles Monœcus (Monaco). To decide between these conflicting claims is impossible; and it may well be that, during the decline of the Phœnicians, the Greeks went ahead and took their place.

What is certain is that the chief impulse to the life of Massilia came from Phocæa. The men of Phocæa, a town in the north-west of Asia Minor, were among the most adventurous of the Ionian Greeks. Indeed, there are touches of romance about their founding of Massilia. First, they turned to good use the strange experiences of a Samian merchant, named Kolaios. According to Herodotus, he set sail from Samos in 630 B.C. with a cargo for barter or sale in Egypt; but the terrible Euroclydon caught him on the way, as later it was to catch St Paul; and he far outdid the apostle in the length of his compulsory run westwards; for the story goes that that easterly gale drove Kolaios right through the Strait of Calpé, and outside, in the Ocean, he made land in Tarshish. There, says Herodotus, the Samian sold his cargo at considerable profit; and, on regaining his home, out of gratitude for his lucky accident, he placed in the temple of Hera a colossal tripod of bronze, adorned with griffins' heads, worth six talents.[1]

Now, this happy mishap of Kolaios turned the

[1] Herodotus, IV, 152. Clerc (*Massalia*, I, 84) accepts the story.

attention of the Ionian Greeks towards the Western Mediterranean. Possibly, the Phocæans first traded in Tarshish, and then crept back north-eastwards towards the Rhone, and so lit on the site of Massilia.[1] Or, more probably, they approached it through the Tyrrhene Sea. In either case, they founded Massilia soon after 600 B.C.

Here again we meet with romance. The historian Justin relates that the first shipload of Phocæans received a cordial welcome from a neighbouring Ligurian king, perhaps because he was about to let his daughter choose a husband and was not sorry to widen the field of choice. In the ensuing competition the sea won; for when all the suitors, including the Phocæan headmen, came in to the feast, the girl at once presented the conjugal cup to their chief, Euxenos. Hence the early alliance between the Phocæan colonists of Massilia and the neighbouring Ligurian tribe. So runs the story; and, as the Phocæans were fine bold seamen, with a dash of the pirate in them, I see no reason for rejecting it because it is romantic.

Doubtless the pressure of the Persian advance westwards on the coast of Asia Minor sent other Phocæans flying to liberty in the West. But it was the increase of trade up the Rhone Valley which chiefly helped on the growth of Massilia. That trade

[1] See Carpenter, R., *The Greeks in Spain* (Longmans & Co., 1925), especially ch. iii, § 3 for the "Massiliot Sailing-book".

route is one of the great natural routes of the world;
for water carriage up the Rhone and Saône offers
easy access to Central Gaul; and there, not far from
the modern Dijon, is the easiest passage into the
valley of the Seine. The Paris-Lyons-Marseille main
line follows pretty closely the course of the ancient
British and Gallic traders who brought the tin,
lead, and corn of Britain, perhaps also the amber
of the northern coasts, up into Central Gaul and
thence down the Saône and the Rhone to the Mediterranean lands. It was the easiest trade route then, and
is the easiest trade route still, between the English
Channel and the Mediterranean. Massilia taps its
southern end; for the mouth of the Rhone is blocked
with mud-banks; and Massilia is the nearest good
harbour then as now. Early in her history she is
said to have beaten the Carthaginians at sea.[1]

There is singularly little competition in ports
thereabouts. The mouths of the Rhone may be ruled
out as of little use owing to quick silting up with mud;
and other posts east of Massilia are too far from that
river valley to get its trade easily. Massilia therefore has an astonishing combination of advantages;
and the only wonder is that it did not become the
greatest port of the world. We find traces of its
prosperity in the number of early Massiliete coins
discovered at many trading posts far into Gaul and
even as far to the north-east as Tirol. Massilia sent

[1] Thucydides, i, 13.

out colonies as far as the coasts of Spain. Phocæans also for a time were planted at Alalia (Aleria) in Corsica, probably to serve as a link with their communications with Massilia. Their colony in Corsica brought them into sharp collision with Carthage and Etruria, which made common cause to expel it. Hence the first-known battle in the West Mediterranean (537 B.C.) somewhere off Corsica. The Massilietes claimed the victory, but owing to exhaustion abandoned Corsica. Later on, dread of Carthage and Etruria made these isolated Greeks seek the friendship of Rome.[1]

Perhaps the most remarkable proof of the maritime energy of Massilia was afforded by her despatch of the explorer, Pytheas, to discover an all-sea route to the lands whence tin and amber came. He set forth to explore the north-western seas in the year 330 B.C., when Alexander the Great was conquering Persia; and the two enterprises represent the supreme efforts of the Greek genius to compass the world. Concerning that of Pytheas we know little, and that only at second hand. But he is said to have touched at Gades and then coasted along the Atlantic shores of Spain and Gaul, and even to have reached Britain, finally voyaging far into the North Sea, doubtless in search of amber. His effort concerns us here only in so far as it throws doubt on the alleged deadly

[1] For the Carthaginian-Etruscan thalassocracy see Homo, L., *Primitive Italy* (Eng. ed.), pp. 103–5.

hostility of the Phœnicians to all Greek efforts in the West; and also because it illustrates the boundless energy of the Massilietes in seeking to explore the hitherto dreaded Ocean.

No more fruitful alliance took place in the ancient world than that between Rome and Massilia. Its benefits to Rome will soon appear; but also the victory of the Romans in the Punic Wars meant everything for Massilia. And we may frankly admit that in no part of the world was the Roman victory more beneficial than in South Gaul. By this time Massilia had colonized Agatha (Agde) and Rhoda (Rosas) to the West, also Olbia (Hyères Is.), Antipolis (Antibes) and Nicæa (Nice) to the East. Consequently Greek civilization began to spread along South Gaul and the coast of the wild Ligurian tribes. In fact Massilia did much to accustom the natives of South Gaul to a settled life and to habits of commerce; and through her went forth the first civilizing influences in Gaul.

Massilia was a free city, allied to, but of course dependent on, Rome, and enjoyed an immense trade and great prosperity. Siding with Pompey against Cæsar, it held out against Cæsar not only on land but at sea with the fleet. The Massiliete fleet fought bravely, but their allies fled and caused their defeat. The city held out long against Cæsar's forces but finally had to surrender. It was, however, treated by him generously, though it lost some territory and some cherished privileges. "It preserved its independence and its Hellenism in the modest proportions of a provincial town".[1]

If we look ahead we shall see that Cæsar's conquest of Gaul tended finally to increase the intercourse of that land with Italy. Further, when Cæsar Augustus founded the Empire he soon perceived what wealth Gaul would bring to his long-harassed realm. He visited Gaul often and fostered its trade with Italy. The conquest was now clinched in true Roman fashion by the making of harbours and roads. The chief new harbours were Forum Julii (Fréjus) for the imperial fleet and Arelate (Arles) for trade.[2]

Thus, for the first time, the natural resources of Gaul had free play. Tribalism almost vanished, and political and commercial union opened up the land, so that its export of grain to exhausted Italy was immense. Velleius Paterculus states that Gaul sent to Rome as much as Egypt did, and that Gaul and Egypt were the richest provinces of the Empire. Gaul also rivalled Egypt in the export of flax and linen. That industry had been confined to the East, but it now spread westwards to Gaul.[3] Pliny wrote: "All Gaul makes sails, till their enemies

[1] Mommsen, *Provinces of the Roman Empire*, I, 79.
[2] *Ibid.* I, 86.
[3] Ferrero, G., *Greatness and Decline of Rome*, IV, 179; V, 113, 126.

beyond the Rhine imitate them. Gallic linen is more beautiful to the eyes than are their women". The brave tribe of the Nervii in North Gaul made very fine linen cloth, which the weavers of far off Laodicea finally imitated! Indeed Gaul now became the first of manufacturing nations.[1] What a tribute to the unifying power of Rome! Pliny also wrote that Gallic dyers imitated the so-called Tyrian purple by vegetable dyes, but they would not wash! It further appears that Gauls worked mines of the precious metals and were skilled jewellers. In fact Gaul became very rich chiefly owing to her immense trade with Rome, which probably went on mainly by sea for heavy products. Consequently, all parts of Gaul, except the north-west, became Romanized.

Probably on no part of the ancient world did that process confer greater benefits. Mere governmental decrees would not have brought about this change. It was the merchant, the sailor, the corn-grower, the herdsman, the weaver, the miner, the vine-grower, who made Gaul an essential part of Roman life; and the quickest intercourse was by sea. We have no statistics as to the number of ships sailing yearly between Gaul and Italy, but its importance may be judged by the stationing of part of the Roman navy at Forum Julii. Its withdrawal at a later date implies the suppression of piracy in the North-west Mediterranean. In truth, during those four centuries of the

[1] Ferrero, G., *Greatness and Decline of Rome*, v, 343.

Roman occupation, Western Europe gained a cultural and commercial unity which nothing could efface.

The substitution of Roman for Carthaginian rule in North Libya was also destined to bring far-reaching changes. For, as Rome acquired the sea empire of her great rival, she had to remain a great sea power, through fear that Carthage might revive. Mommsen has well said: "The Romans held fast the territory of Carthage...less in order to develop it for their own benefit than to prevent it benefiting others; not to awaken new life there, but to watch the dead body. It was fear and envy which created the (Roman) province of Africa".[1] This is a severe criticism, but it is just. Accordingly, there is little to say about commerce for some 100 years after the destruction of Carthage: "Under the Republic it had not a history. The war with Jugurtha was only a lion hunt".[2]

Not until the end of the civil war between Cæsar and Pompey did the Roman province of "Africa" greatly expand. In 46 B.C. (i.e. just 100 years after the destruction of Carthage) Cæsar put down the last efforts of the Pompeians in that land. Thereafter he began to enlarge the bounds of "Africa", until, finally, in later decades, it comprised even the kingdom of Mauretania.

[1] Mommsen, *The Provinces of the Roman Empire*, II, 306.
[2] *Ibid.* II, 306.

Probably the chief reason for this extension of Roman rule was the need of further supplies of corn for Italy. Italian agriculture had long been going downhill. The causes of the decline are traceable to the terrible drain on the population of rural Italy caused by the Punic and Macedonian Wars, soon to be followed by the long succession of civil wars and proscriptions. Indeed Rome was largely the victim of her own victorious campaigns. She had conquered too many rich lands and too easily. Hence the rise of a coarse and brutal luxury, which depended largely on slaves. First, slaves came from Sardinia (*Sardi venales* became a byword for a glut in the market), and with them came Sardinian corn. There came also Sicilian corn. Then the frightful misgovernment of these and other provinces by official robbers like Verres, ruined these lands, and for a time depleted the yield of corn, especially in Sicily. Italy now must have foreign corn: and, as her slave population could not, or would not, get the corn out of her hard-worked soil, it had to come from lands further afield: the chief of these were Gaul, "Africa", and finally Egypt.

It seems strange that "Africa" should beat Italy at corn-growing. But so it was. Parts of North Africa are, even now, very good corn land. They were even more so then. Professor Albertini, formerly of the University of Algiers, states that in the plain of Sousse, some 60 miles south of Tunis, there were natural phosphates so rich as to produce the heaviest wheat crops in the world. They excelled even those of the Nile valley. The Sousse wheat yielded 150 for 1, while Egyptian wheat yielded only 100 for 1.[1]

Thus Rome's conquest of Carthage finally had the effect of completing the ruin of Italian agriculture. Naturally, the cheap and abundant corn of "Africa" kept busy a whole fleet of grain ships which freighted from Sousse, Carthage, Utica, the two Hippos and several smaller ports, as far west as Melilla. We know little or nothing about the details of this trade; but the numbers of the ports and the vast wealth of land-holders in "Africa"[2] show that the trade must have been immense. Many privileges were accorded to Roman wheat merchants and shippers; and great though futile efforts were put forth to construct a suitable port at Ostia, the mouth of the Tiber. Later, Puteoli served that purpose.

Wheat and barley were not the only objects of export from "Africa". Rome procured from that province most of the lions, leopards and elephants needed for her games in the amphitheatres. Indeed the great felines thus supplied were popularly called "Africans". How Rome got them across the sea is an unsolved mystery. She also obtained thence

[1] Albertini, M., *L'Afrique romaine*, Lecture III.
[2] Ferrero, *Greatness and Decline of Rome*, v, 341. Nero executed six African land-holders to seize their wealth (Pliny, *Nat. Hist.* XVIII, 6).

building stone, marble, dates, fruit and vegetables, and great quantities of wood for heating houses and baths. In fact, the Romans made the best possible use of that great province: they were careful to conserve water power by damming up torrents and thus forming reservoirs, and they used the power thus stored up for hydraulic purposes. Professor Albertini states that, even to-day, the French regime has not equalled that of the Romans in regard to the conservation and use of water power.[1]

Now, all this energy implies a great and regular trade between Italy and "Africa". Of its details we know next to nothing; but we infer from the many proofs of interchange that in the early empire that commerce must have been very great.

Probably its growth enriched the ports of South Italy, which were still Greek in population and in sentiment. Their reliance on this trade may have been one of the chief factors binding them to the Roman connection, which was assured by the presence of a Roman fleet at Misenum, near Neapolis.[2]

The most valuable of Rome's acquisitions from Carthage was Spain. That land had formed both the treasury and the recruiting ground of Hannibal for his attack. Hence the vigour and pertinacity of the Roman counterstrokes. They could hardly have suc-

---

[1] Albertini, Lecture III.
[2] Heitland, W. E., *Roman Republic*, II, 423, 433.

ceeded but for the help rendered by Punic-hating Massilia and her daughter cities named above. These provided shelter and refreshment for the Roman fleets, from Nicæa in the east to Rhoda and Agatha in North Spain. What this meant to great fleets of row-boats in that stormiest part of the Mediterranean cannot now be realized. The Romans, in order to shorten the march round into Spain took ship at Pisa, and thereby avoided the rough and dangerous coast track round the Ligurian Gulf, beset as it was by the wild folk of the hinterland.[1] They would arrive at Nicæa and Massilia more or less exhausted and would need a thorough rest there or on landing at their destination at Tarraco. Without Massiliete help Rome would probably never have conquered Spain. Once on that open eastern coast, her troops had the advantage of mobility over the defenders, and could choose their point of attack. Hence their comparatively easy conquest of Spain, which has always been most vulnerable on her eastern coast.

The policy of Rome towards Gades (probably the most ancient city in Western Europe) was wise. She accorded to it the privileges of a free city; and apparently the city prospered; for it was one of the few Phœnician ports which survived these stormy years intact. At any rate, Gades remained prosperous for many generations, and Strabo testifies to its wealth and enterprise.[2]

[1] Livy, xxxvii, 57.   [2] Strabo, iii, 168.

The rest of Spain was far less fortunate. Roman rule soon proved to be heavier than that of Carthage; and Livy himself admits that the Spaniards found they had now fallen under a worse bondage.[1] In fact under the Republic the government of Rome in Spain was brutal. She seems to have recouped herself from Spanish mines and vineyards for her terrible losses in the Hannibalic War. Polybius, when he visited New Carthage, estimated that there were 40,000 slaves at work in the silver mines near that city.[2] Rome reserved for herself the Spanish gold mines; but other mines she sold to private individuals.[3] She also extorted a heavy tribute, especially in corn. In fact, Spain was bled so severely that a long succession of wars and rebellions occurred. In these the Romans were often defeated and lost heavily, though in the end their command of the sea and pertinacity prevailed. For more than a century the rule of the great Republic was seen at its worst in Spain and Sicily. In fact, the prosperity of these new possessions must have been seriously impaired by the greed and tyranny of Roman proconsuls. But the Emperors introduced a severe supervision over Roman governors; and under the Empire both Sicily and Spain recovered their prosperity amidst the general peace so favourable to all Mediterranean lands.

[1] Livy, xxxiv, 18.   [2] Polybius, xxxiv, 9.
[3] Ferrero, v, 341.

The Balearic Isles now proved to be very useful links in the new maritime Empire, both for the encouragement of commerce and the suppression of piracy. The Carthaginian admiral, Mago, had given his name to that excellent harbour in Minorca, now known as Port Mahon; under Rome, as under Carthage, it formed an important central station commanding the West Mediterranean, and encouraged mariners to venture on the direct voyage from Spain to Italy, or from "Africa" to Massilia.[1]

To sum up: By conquering and destroying Carthage, the Romans were able to enter into the rich heritage of her colonial Empire, which comprised the north coast of Libya, the coastal provinces of Spain, the Balearic Isles, and the scattered Phœnician posts in the Western Mediterranean and Atlantic. Roman sea power and Roman law now bound together all the lands bordering that sea in something like unity. Of course that unity was for a long time only political and governmental; but even that meant much. For, be it remembered, under Rome the coast of "Africa", later the haunt of corsairs, hummed with peaceful commerce. Merchants could trade between Utica and Massilia, Tunes and

---

[1] See R. Carpenter, *op. cit.* pp. 18, 48, on the times of Greek and Punic occupations of parts of the Balearic Isles as links (along with N. Sardinia) in the short route from Magna Græcia to N.E. Spain. He assigns priority to Greek seamen on their way to Callipolis (Tarragona).

Neapolis, Ostia and New Carthage or Gades, with the certainty of finding Roman warships to protect them afloat and in the last resort Roman justice to guarantee their dealings ashore. No wonder that commerce increased, or that the Roman language began to replace Phœnician, Greek, Numidian, and Iberian throughout this vast area; so that, under the better colonial rule of the Roman Empire, what was at first only a political unity became a cultural unity. We hear very much about the influence of Roman roads in promoting Roman civilization; but the influence of Roman fleets in bringing about that miracle has been almost entirely ignored. Yet it is demonstrable that the Roman Empire depended quite as much on its fleets as on its roads.

CHAPTER V

ROMAN SUPREMACY IN THE EASTERN MEDITERRANEAN

In the last chapter I raised the question whether the spread of Roman power over the eastern world was the result of deep-laid design; and I deferred to this chapter an examination of the evidence, which has too often been interpreted off-hand and without due reference to the naval factor.

In this connection it is well to remember that Italy turns, as it were, her back and her heel on the East; and that her long harbourless Adriatic coast discourages action in that quarter. Rome faces westwards; her early interests lay in the Tyrrhene Sea; and her long struggle with Carthage turned her energies imperiously towards Sicily, Africa and Spain. Down to the year 200 B.C. she had no energy to spare for extensive oriental designs. In fact, we now approach the question whether her eastern conquests did not arise out of events which could not be foreseen, yet had to be met as the occasion arose.

Consider first her acquisition of control over the Adriatic Sea. It came about not long after the First Punic War, but only as a result of great provocations from the pirates of the Illyrian coast. These pirates had for ages harried the commerce and the coasts of East Italy and of Epirus. They had as places of refuge the many islands of the Adriatic; for intricate archipelagos form the breeding places of pirates; and from these islands they preyed on all neighbouring cities and their traders. When Rome founded the colony of Brundisium (244 B.C.) she soon felt the pin-pricks of these intolerable thieves. But she was not much concerned with commerce. It is noteworthy that the protests about piracy in the Adriatic came from Brundisium and Tarentum, not from Rome. But she now intervened on behalf of the mercantile cities of Magna Græcia so as to revive their commerce with Epirus and the Hellenistic States. These last were in a forlorn condition since they were beaten by the pirates of the Adriatic in a pitched battle, and lost to them Corcyra (Corfu). The outrages of the pirates indeed passed all bounds; and when Rome sent two envoys to protest, the Illyrian Queen, Teuta, scoffingly remarked that according to their law piracy was a lawful form of trade. The younger of the envoys retorted that the Romans would help her to improve Illyrian law—a sarcasm which cost both envoys their lives (230 B.C.).

Rome answered this insolent defiance by sending a fleet of 200 galleys into the Adriatic. It carried all before it, driving the pirates off the sea and then burning out their nests ashore. For the first time, probably, in all history the Adriatic was made safe for commerce. This stern and masterful action was a lesson, not only to Illyrian pirates but also to bickering Greeks, whose weakness had of late exposed them to that disgraceful defeat from the pirates. Evidently a new power was coming into the East, a power, which, at the first great naval effort ended for the time a sea curse which had brooded for ages over the Adriatic. Rome also assured safety for the growing commerce of Magna Græcia in the Ionian Sea by gaining a protectorate over that part of Illyria which is opposite the heel of Italy. It included good ports like Epidamnus (Dyrrachium), Apollonia and Aulon. She also occupied the islands of Pharos in the mid-Adriatic and Corcyra which commanded its entrance. Thus she became the chief naval power in the Adriatic and Ionian Seas, and therefore a rival of the Macedonian kingdom.

Naturally, both Philip V of Macedon and the Greek States became apprehensive of the spread eastwards of the Roman power, though there are grounds for thinking that the Roman Senate had no desire for conquering either of those peoples. The Senate acted by no means aggressively towards Philip or the Greeks. In fact, the provocation came from Philip. It arose out of the Second Punic War; for Rome's difficulties during that war led Philip, after the Battle of Trasimene, to seek to chastise those Illyrians who had become allies of Rome. He even seized their coast towns. But he had no fleet; and though he set about building one, yet it was too weak and too raw to challenge betimes the force which Rome contrived to keep in those waters.

He had one chance. It occurred in 216, not long before Cannæ. He then managed to bring round from Thessalonica and other Macedonian ports a force of 100 light craft, which sailed up the Ionian Sea in order to overpower the then rather depleted force which the Romans had on the Illyrian coast. But the allies of Rome informed her of this move; and her commander in Sicilian waters at once despatched ten quinqueremes as a reinforcement. Rumour magnified their numbers; and Philip's 100 light craft turned tail and fled to Cephallenia. Polybius censures their action, and I think rightly; for Philip's effort was a great one; and no determined leader abandons such an effort without good evidence that the force nearing him is overwhelming. Philip believed a mere rumour, took no steps to examine it, and himself actually returned to Macedonia. How different the future of the world might have been if he had crippled the Romans in a great naval battle in that critical year of Cannæ! If he had then gained command of the Ionian and Adriatic Seas, he could have sent over to Italy a large well-disciplined force to help Hannibal; and that force might have turned the balance against Rome.

Owing to Philip's naval fiasco things went very differently; for Rome retained the mastery at sea. Now, one great advantage of sea power is that it enables a State to take the offensive when and where it chooses. Henceforth, with rare exceptions, it was Rome which could attack Macedon, not Macedon Rome. The result was seen in the helplessness of Philip in the closing stages of the Hannibalic War; for though he made a secret treaty of alliance with Hannibal in the spring of 215, yet not having mastery at sea, he could not get troops across to Italy. In fact, Rome, scenting the danger, ordered the prætor commanding her fleet at Tarentum to watch the entrance of the Adriatic with 50 warships carrying troops on board; and if Philip threatened to invade Italy, the prætor was to forestall him by an attack on the Illyrian coast.

This wise policy saved Rome from the Macedonian danger; for when Philip did capture Oricus in the Gulf of Aulon, the prætor struck at him, recovered the place, and chased the Macedonian forces from that seaboard. Philip, without waiting for a Punic fleet to come and help him, burnt his light craft and retreated eastwards into Macedonia. Roman firmness, then, dispelled the Macedonian thundercloud of war, which receded over the mountains. That all-important coastline remained in the hands of Rome and her allies.

To these allies was now added the Ætolian League; for Philip offended that League and other Greek States, thus driving them into the arms of Rome. The victorious Roman fleet appeared in the Gulf of Corinth, and received a hearty welcome from the cities of the Ætolian League north of that gulf.

A Roman-Ætolian treaty was formed, while Philip gained the help of the Achæan League south of that gulf.

Into the details of this complicated struggle it would be wearisome to enter. All that we need note is that Roman sea power, though not effectively or even vigorously used, brought about a stalemate in the year 205. All the combatants were exhausted, or disgusted with their allies; and, as at that time Rome had not yet quite finished with Carthage, she alienated her Ætolian allies by deserting them, and left Philip aggrandized at the expense of them and of the Illyrians. But the main fact is that Rome backed out of this First Macedonian War (which for her was a secondary issue) without any great loss on the Illyrian coast, and she left her allies to bear the losses. Meanwhile she gathered up her strength for the final effort against Carthage. Her fleet had saved her from defeat in the East; and it is clear from the shabby way in which she treated her Greek allies, and in which she shuffled out of that war, that she had no definite eastern policy.[1]

After finishing with Carthage in 201 B.C., Rome turned sharply against Philip and sent him a clear challenge. The occasion was inviting; for he had made a secret compact with Antiochus III ("the Great"), King of Syria, with a view to the partition of the moribund kingdom of Egypt and its posses-

[1] *Camb. Ancient Hist.* VIII, 136.

sions in the Cyclades, and on the coasts of Asia Minor and Syria. While Antiochus prepared to strike at the nearer possessions of Egypt Philip set upon those nearer him in Asia Minor, and, with a fleet which he had of late constructed, attacked and captured Samos, where he incorporated several Egyptian vessels in his new fleet. His progress on that coast alarmed and enrolled against him Attalus, King of the rising and already considerable kingdom of Pergamum (nearly opposite Lesbos) and the powerful island of Rhodes. After indecisive battles against these two States, they appealed to Rome for help against him.

What should the Roman Senate do in this case? The Roman people were exhausted and war-weary with the long struggle against Hannibal. And what was this eastern question to them? Nothing, so it seemed. Yet the Senate contrived to bring about the rupture with Philip, though it had no grievance against him. Clearly, it had resolved to make him pay dearly for his conduct in the former war, so tamely ended. Now Rome might easily wreak her revenge. Philip was campaigning with doubtful prospects far away in Asia Minor. His communications with Macedonia were hazardous; for the fleets of Pergamum and Rhodes, added to the sea power of Rome, might cut him off altogether from his homeland by severing that crucial link the Hellespont crossing. On military grounds, then, it was well to strike at a rival or enemy who had committed the worst of strategic blunders in exposing his rear to a telling blow at that strait, where empires were made and unmade, the Hellespont. And it will be well for the student of naval history to note the skill with which Rome utilized that strategic world centre, and the stupidity with which her enemies yielded it to her grasp.

Accordingly the Senate welcomed the appeals of Attalus and the Rhodians. It went further and ordered Philip to refrain from attacking any Greek State—an order which was a calculated insult to a successor of the mighty Alexander. The insult was felt the more keenly by Philip because he conceived himself to have great cause for complaint against the Ætolians and Athens. The real cause for this Second Macedonian War was that Rome, Pergamum and Rhodes could, and soon did, muster an overpowering fleet, and might expect to cut off Philip from Europe, also to overpower the Achæan League which still held to the Macedonian alliance.[1]

Rome did not realize the whole of this far-reaching programme. For, first, Philip succeeded in crossing the Hellespont and so made his way back in haste to Macedon. But her fleet, strengthened by those of Pergamum and Rhodes, carried all before it on the coasts of Greece. So great was the allied force as to impose neutrality on the Achæan League—a terrible

[1] *Camb. Ancient Hist.* VIII, 157–64.

loss to Philip; for it meant the loss of that warlike genius, Philopœmen, who had led the Achæan forces to many triumphs. Naval supremacy also doubled the energy of the Ætolian League on behalf of Rome.

The result was seen in her decisive victory of Cynoscephalæ in the south of Thessaly, where Philip lost 13,000 men out of his 25,500 (197 B.C.). In the sequel the Romans expelled Philip from all his possessions in Greece and in Greek Asia Minor, and thenceforth garrisoned several of his possessions in Asia Minor and the Ægean, including Abydos. Thus ended this unjust war. The Roman proconsul, Flamininus, now declared Greece freed from all control by Philip and virtually under the protection of Rome, but she withdrew her garrisons. Thus, at one stride, she gained supremacy in the East of Europe, and now found herself face to face with Antiochus, King of Syria.

The career of that monarch is an enigma. Former historians represented him as a typical oriental tyrant, spoilt by early adulation, then by easy successes over decadent Egypt, and now betraying his former partner in crime, Philip V, when fallen upon evil days. This lurid picture has been toned down by recent researchers,[1] who throw strong Syrian sidelights on this western presentation. We cannot enter here into these tangled questions, but must let the outstanding

[1] E.g. Holleaux, Prof. M., in *Camb. Ancient Hist.* VIII, chap. 7, pt. 2.

facts speak for themselves. In brief they are as follows:

In the course of the long struggles between Syria and Egypt (the aggrandized Egypt which now held parts of Syria, Asia Minor and the Cyclades), Antiochus planned, with the help of Philip, to overthrow that decadent power and seize most of the spoils. When Philip's campaign in Asia Minor brought about the Roman intervention aforesaid, and his own condign defeat, Syrian forces proceeded both to seize the spoils which he now must drop, and also to occupy Macedonian posts on the Hellespont and the nearer parts of Thrace (196 B.C.), which had once belonged to Seleucus, ancestor of Antiochus.

Rome regarded these moves as a prelude to an attack upon her protectorate over the Greeks, whose resentment against "barbarian" control was rapidly rising. Therefore Antiochus, knowing of her difficulties in North Italy and Spain, and reassured by the marriage contract of his daughter Cleopatra with Ptolemy V of Egypt, turned a deaf ear to Roman demands that he should free the Ionian Greek cities lately seized by him and refrain from all action in Europe. These demands, however, earned for Rome the friendship, and later the active co-operation, of Philip of Macedon, but failed to enlist the hoped for support of all the Greeks. In the sequel Athens and the Achæan League sided with Rome, while the powerful Ætolian League and Thessaly made common cause with Antiochus, who now proclaimed himself liberator of the Greeks. With the resources of Syria, the half of Greece, nearly the whole of Asia Minor, and also of Egypt, on his side, he had good chances of success in case of a rupture with Rome.

Meanwhile, the situation had been complicated by the arrival at his Court of Ephesus of that eternal enemy of Rome, Hannibal. Failing to stir up exhausted Carthage to one more effort, the great leader made his way to Tyre, and thence to Ephesus late in 195 B.C. He came as an exile, not as a coadjutor in a scheme for a world war; but his presence rendered the Romans more suspicious, therefore more exigent; and the tone of Antiochus hardened somewhat when the greatest of generals was at his side, and held out the prospect of naval succours from Tyre and Sidon, perhaps even from Carthage. Gradually, the Roman-Syrian dispute, exacerbated by mutual suspicions, tended towards a rupture, which was hastened by preparations that were nominally defensive. The Roman Senate, fearing a Carthaginian-Syrian attack on Sicily, pressed on the construction of 70 quinqueremes, and assembled a large army in South Italy.[1] Antiochus long wavered, but, resolving to anticipate their arrival in Greece, set sail thither in the early autumn of 192 with 10,000 foot, 500 horse, and 6 elephants, in a fleet of 100 warships and 200 transports.

[1] *Camb. Ancient Hist.* VIII, 206, 207.

The arrival of this paltry force (albeit announced as merely a vanguard) gave pause to the expectant Ætolians and heartened all pro-Roman Greeks; and when the forces of Rome and Macedon marched against Antiochus and his Ætolian allies, the issue could not be doubtful. In the final fight, at Thermopylæ, his left wing posted on the inland heights was broken by a flank attack like that on Leonidas and his Spartans, and the whole Syrian force fled in rout (April, 191 B.C.). Collecting 500 men at Chalcis Antiochus set sail for Ephesus, leaving the Ætolians to wage an obstinate but hopeless campaign against the might of Rome.

Meanwhile the value of her alliances with Pergamum and Rhodes was clearly shown; for 24 Pergamene warships, joining 75 Roman in the Ægean, assured a complete victory over 70 well-equipped Syrian ships off the Corycus peninsula; and when 25 Rhodians joined the victors, the vanquished fled to the harbour of Ephesus. Early in 190 a Rhodian admiral was surprised in the harbour of Samos and lost all but seven of his fleet. This disaster rendered impossible the crossing of the Ægean by the Roman army, especially as the Phœnician reinforcements, lately collected by Hannibal, were expected in that sea. But the roundabout march through Thrace to the Hellespont had several advantages; for Philip's help expedited that effort and weighted the blow against the fortresses of Antiochus on the Hellespont. Moreover, before that blow fell, the skilled Rhodian fleet, watching for Hannibal off the coast of Pamphylia, defeated his large but ill-disciplined force—the only time he fought against Rome at sea. Again the brave islanders displayed their resourcefulness in the final decisive contest, which took place in August off Myonnesus and the Corycus peninsula.[1] At the outset the Syro-Phœnician fleet gained some advantages, until the Rhodian wing discomfited the Asiatics opposite by charging with poles thrust out holding pans of burning pitch which was poured upon the hostile crews. The Romans also broke the Syrian centre, and, charging back on it, completed the victory. With the loss of 42 ships the fleet of Antiochus fled to Ephesus, where it was blockaded.

News of this disaster led him hastily to withdraw his garrison from Lysimachia, the military key to the Thracian Chersonese; and equally tame retreats of the defenders of neighbouring seaports on the Hellespont enabled the Roman army under the Scipios to capture with ease those keys of Europe, and to cross over that strait into Asia. The Pergamene alliance now aided the ever-fortunate Scipios to march rapidly southwards; and the final conflict took place, early in 189, at Magnesia, south-east of Ephesus. Perhaps it was anxiety to save his fleet, blocked in that harbour, which led the Syrian monarch to stake all at Magnesia. But his conglomerate force could

[1] For details see Livy, xxxvii, 29, 30.

not withstand the impact of the disciplined Romans, who scattered it in flight with the loss, it is said, of 50,000 men. Thereupon the crews of the Syro-Phœnician fleet, shut in at Ephesus, stole away by land, leaving the ships as a prize to the victors. Utterly dispirited, Antiochus laid down his arms.

Professor Holleaux has pointed out the lavish gifts of Fortune to the Romans in these crucial years —only thirteen after their defeat of Carthage.[1] Certainly Fortune did favour them. But I agree with Polybius that their good fortune resulted from their good sense. Their prompt action and skilful use of serviceable allies are above praise. Also I am more impressed by the unwisdom of Antiochus than by the favour of the fickle goddess to Rome. That monarch committed blunder after blunder. First, his attack on Thrace, besides being strategically unsound, threw Philip into the arms of Rome. Next, his aim of arousing all the Greeks against Rome was frustrated by the despatch of far too few troops and too small a supporting fleet. Thirdly, when driven from Thermopylæ, he abandoned the Greeks so precipitately as to discourage them and all his troops. For the defence of Asia Minor he needed to hold firmly the Hellespont with an army and a great fleet. He did not do so. He scattered his forces and made so ineffective a use of his fleet that the Romans and their allies easily secured the keys of the Hellespont

[1] *Camb. Ancient Hist.* viii, 215, 224.

and mastery of the Ægean. Finally, when Rome and her allies had a good grip on the Ægean Sea and the west coast of Asia Minor, Antiochus offered battle near Ephesus; whereas, by retreating into the interior of Asia Minor he could have increased greatly the difficulties of the Roman and allied forces, now dependent on naval supplies. Instead, he staked everything on a pitched battle near the coast. He deserved his overthrow quite as much as Philip V of Macedon had done. Both blundered by carrying their arms into alien continents without holding firmly the fortresses on the Hellespont. The loss of these broke their backs, just as the threat of such a loss broke the will to war of Xerxes after Salamis.

The Romans also owed their eastern successes largely to their timely alliances with the sea powers, Rhodes and Pergamum, which afforded the Roman fleet excellent bases in the Ægean and rendered yeoman service in the battles. By the year 189 Rome and her allies virtually controlled the Eastern Mediterranean; and soon had Greeks and Phœnicians, Syrians and Egyptians, in the hollow of her hand. Let it suffice to recall that strange incident of the year 168 B.C. near the mouth of the Nile. A very commonplace Roman, Popillius Lænas, who was sent by the Senate to order Antiochus IV (Epiphanes) to evacuate Egypt, did so in the following brusque but decisive manner. Meeting that great monarch in the open, and finding him bent on the conquest of

Egypt, the Roman simply drew a circle around him on the sand and forbade him to move from it until he had promised to refrain from that act. The Syrian monarch actually obeyed this insolent demand, and was then allowed to move. He then did evacuate Egypt.[1]

We need not follow the later extensions of Roman power eastwards. They resulted naturally from their easy triumph in the years 200–189 B.C. In these chapters I select only the crucial events which illustrate the importance of the naval factor; and when Rome became mistress of the Eastern Mediterranean, her further conquests of Asia Minor, Syria and Egypt were a natural sequel to her triumphant action against that feeblest of "great" kings, Antiochus III.

The final conquest of Greece by Rome, especially the brutal sack of Corinth by Mummius in 146 B.C., were signs that she was by that time determined to control the East Mediterranean, and to crush that possibly rival city. The fact that these events in the East occurred in the same year as her still more savage destruction of Carthage proves her resolve to control absolutely both the West and the East Mediterranean. We may note here the revival of Corinth as an Italian colony, which was effected by Julius Cæsar. Owing to the natural advantages of

[1] Heitland, *The Roman Republic*, ii, 116; Cary, M., *The Greek World* (323–146 B.C.), p. 218.

position Corinth soon revived; and its cosmopolitan populace became noted for coarse and extravagant luxury.

Of far greater interest is the story of the island of Rhodes. In times when the feuds of the Greeks naturally brought them under the supremacy of Rome, it is comforting to find at least one Greek island maintaining its liberty and prosperity. Here again good fortune was due mainly to good sense. That quality had long characterized the Rhodians. Two and a half centuries earlier their three chief towns, previously rivals, had displayed it by agreeing to unite in the common effort of founding as capital the city of Rhodes on the triple bays at the northeast tip of the island. That city, well situated and well fortified, soon became great; and the island prospered for centuries, largely owing to the skill and daring of its seamen. "Ten Rhodians are worth ten ships" ran a Greek proverb.[1] Further, its rulers sought, like the Venetians of a later age, to frame alliances with the leading power of the time. This mercantile opportunism enabled Rhodes to steer her way through the wars which wrecked the Greek States; and now, when the Romans spread their power eastwards, Rhodes bowed before them. She had to surrender several disputed points in a treaty of alliance with her overbearing partner (165 B.C.).[2]

[1] Torr, *Rhodes in Ancient Times*, p. 27.
[2] *Camb. Ancient Hist.* VIII, 289–91.

Among other things Rome declared Delos a free port under her protection, and it became a keen competitor with Rhodes. Nevertheless Rhodes remained a great centre of commerce. In fact, the Romans seem to have adopted much of their maritime law from that of Rhodes—witness a reported saying of Antoninus Pius: "Let the matter be judged according to the naval law of the Rhodians, in so far as any of our own laws do not conflict with that".[1] Such was the Roman custom in naval disputes. Thus it seems likely that much maritime law of to-day owes its origin ultimately to that of Rhodes.

Strong in her hold on Greece and on the fortresses of the Bosporus, fortified also by her alliances with Pergamum and Rhodes, Rome now controlled the Eastern Mediterranean. Her supremacy was again to be challenged; for the Greeks remained restive under a yoke which they despised as that of un-cultured "barbarians". Neither did peoples further East look on her thalassocracy as final. All the anti-Roman forces came into full play at the bidding of a powerful and ambitious monarch, Mithridates VI, King of Pontus. Making himself by degrees master of nearly all the lands bordering on the Euxine, he founded what we may term a Euxine Empire, rivalling the eastern possessions of Rome. The forests and the iron of Pontus (the cradle of his

[1] Pandects, xiv, 9; quoted by Torr, p. 52. But see *Camb. Ancient Hist.* viii, 636.

Empire) yielded the materials for building and maintaining a great fleet as well as an army of 100,000 men. With these he sought to overrun the west and south of Asia Minor.

Besides, Mithridates stirred up the Greeks to throw off the yoke of Rome; and as Rome was then (90–80 B.C.) convulsed by civil strifes, her collapse in the East seemed probable. It was averted by the self-sacrificing help of Rhodes and by the services of that great general, Sulla, whose skill and valour prevailed over the Pontic army in Greece in the battles of Chæronea and Orchomenus not far from Athens. Thereupon a Roman-Rhodian fleet restored Roman supremacy in the Ægean and neighbouring waters (85–84 B.C.).

The civil wars and resulting confusions in Rome and Italy gave the Asiatic despot other opportunities for attacking her in Asia Minor; but we cannot enter into the details of the Second and Third Mithridatic Wars. We must, however, notice briefly one of the methods which Mithridates adopted for harassing the Romans and Rhodians at sea. He made systematic use of the pirates who swarmed in the south of Asia Minor.

Piracy is a plague which spreads rapidly in times of civil war and disturbances; for, when men cannot live by honest trade and tillage, they turn naturally to a life of robbery at sea; for there, as we have seen, law could at no time be enforced with ease, and was

everywhere defied when no strong State curbed the
unruly elements. As Italy rocked to and fro in the
civil wars of Marius and Sulla, and Mithridates
terrorized Asia Minor, hordes of despairing or infuriated men took to the "profession of the sea";
and all the efforts of the Rhodians failed to prevent
piracy spreading like a plague. With the aid of
piratical fleets Mithridates gained some successes
over the sea forces of Rome and her allies, and the
lot of Rhodes seemed desperate; for, even if discipline gained the day, the beaten robbers would
retreat and flee to some cliff or mountain fastness
on or near the coasts of Crete, Lydia or Cilicia. In
fact it needed swift and well-armed fleets and a
strong column of lightly equipped troops acting in
concert, to stamp out the piratical pest.

Of course well-armed and disciplined fleets generally prevailed over larger numbers of pirates; but
these generally excelled in speed. Pirates must be
quick if they are to make a living; a slow pirate is
as impossible a creature as a laggard hawk. Pirates
have, indeed, exercised on navigation much the same
influence that raptorial birds exert on other birds,
viz. a general quickening up of pace and keenness of
outlook. But pirates rarely, if ever, built up an
efficient fleet. So in the long run Roman discipline
and Rhodian skill prevailed over these scratch collections of self-seeking marauders. Mithridates lost
command of the sea; and finally a Roman and allied

fleet entered the Euxine and enabled a Roman army to chase Mithridates away from Pontus into exile in Armenia.

Thus ended the fourth challenge which came from the East. In her constant quest for order Rome was brought perforce to the frontiers of Armenia and Parthia, but even there she did not find stability. As Mr Heitland has well said: "Rome was drawn into the tangle of Greek and Eastern affairs; and, once in, she found it impossible to get out; nor could she find a tolerable halting-place till she had established herself as the dominant power in the whole of the Greek-speaking world".[1]

For now came a fifth challenge. An outburst of the piratical pest again threatened her. The flotsam and jetsam of the Mithridatic forces and of their victims now strewed the waters of the Levant with robber squadrons which waxed bolder and bolder, until honest trade almost ceased. Rome, half paralysed by her civil strifes and proscriptions, could for the time do little at sea. Rhodes and Pergamum were overborne; and the West Mediterranean was also stricken by the plague. Sicilians, ruined by Roman proconsuls, and Ligurians ever eager for plunder, rowed forth from their creeks to pounce on the corn ships from Africa or from Massilia, thus rendering the Gallic trade to Italy utterly unsafe. Pirate squadrons banded together to form fleets; and one such fleet

[1] Heitland, *The Roman Republic*, ii, 12.

actually swooped down on Ostia and burnt many warships as well as corn ships. Such was the result of neglecting to keep up an efficient navy.[1]

At last, in 67 B.C., the great city stood on the verge of famine; and the people were stung to action. Gabinius, one of the tribunes of the people, proposed and carried a scheme which established a drastic naval and military dictatorship. From among the consulars the Senate was bidden to select a commander who would have absolute control over the whole of the Mediterranean and its coasts, also as far as 50 miles inland. He was to command 120,000 infantry, 5000 cavalry and 500 ships of war. A sum equal to £1,300,000 was at once to be at his disposal. These proposals of Gabinius infuriated the Senate, but they were carried almost unanimously in the Comitia Tributa. Thus a naval-military dictatorship was set up; and the voice of the people designated Gnæus Pompeius virtually as dictator. Such was the confidence in his ability to enforce these far-reaching powers that the price of corn fell immediately to its ordinary rates. Thus the food problem (intimately connected with the piratical problem) was the means of setting up a dictatorship which pointed the way towards the Empire.

Personal rule was never better justified than by Pompeius. Mommsen and other historians who persistently belittle him ignore the difficulties which

[1] See Ihne (Eng. ed. IV, 112–14) for details.

confronted this dictator of the Mediterranean. But they were immense. Even the Sardinian and Sicilian corn supplies were being held up by pirates, who swarmed even in the Tyrrhene Sea, close to the chief naval base, Misenum. Against these Pompeius first directed his new fleet; and in 40 days he is said to have freed that sea from the pirate pests. This alone was a wonderful achievement in days when warships were as a rule slower than the light piratical craft.

Thereupon Pompeius sailed with 60 of his best ships to the south coasts of Asia Minor. Concerting his plans well with his lieutenants in that area, and doubtless well helped by the Rhodian fleet, he routed the piratical hordes, especially those of Cilicia, chased the fugitives to their strongholds in the Cilician Mountains and stormed them, or else gained their submission by timely clemency. In 49 days (we are told) the Cilician bands were utterly routed, or reclaimed to a life of honesty.[1] To me these two campaigns of 40 days in the West, and 49 days in the East seem suspect. For the 500 Roman warships would need crews of at least 90,000 seamen. How could Rome quickly raise and train this vast number (mostly new) so as to be efficient oarsmen and hunt down pirates, who are nothing if not swift? To do all this over a great extent of sea and coastline was a very difficult and probably lengthy task. The whole

[1] Ormerod (*History of Piracy*, pp. 234–41) accepts the traditional account.

episode shows the cogent effect of combined naval
and military operations, especially in times when
fleets could not for long keep at sea. The Romans,
like Alexander in his siege of Tyre, sought to
conquer the sea by a systematic conquest of the
neighbouring coastline.

Mommsen, indeed, asserts that of course Pompeius and his well-organized warships and troops
easily prevailed over mere pirates—as easily as a
well-organized city police prevails over combined
gangs of thieves.[1] The simile is misleading; for
nearly all thieves are cowards, whereas pirates are
generally desperate men and also skilful seamen,
swift at retreat as at attack; while most of the crews
of Pompeius must have been raw. All credit to them
that they succeeded, whatever the duration of the
campaign. In this gigantic effort (called forth by the
fifth challenge from the East) Rome put forth more
energy than in any of her naval wars, as was natural
seeing that she was fighting the pirates for her vital
supplies of food. Her action at this crisis points the
way to what in all probability we should do if our
food were being almost entirely cut off. In her case
the food crisis led to a dictatorship, which preluded
the Empire.

If we look forward to the period of the Roman
Empire we note that Rome policed the Eastern

[1] Mommsen, iv, 114.

Mediterranean from three chief naval bases. One was behind the Pharos, the island off Alexandria; and the fleet stationed there guarded the very important supplies of grain from Egypt.[1] Another base was Seleucia, to the west of Antioch, guarding the Syrian supplies of grain. The importance of those supplies may be measured by the long tunnels and deep cuttings made through cliffs to a depression behind them, which formed a landlocked harbour at Seleucia on that otherwise difficult coast.[2] The third naval station in the Levant was the Isle of Karpathos, which guarded the middle passage to Italy and the approach to the Ægean. From these three bases went forth the fleets which policed the East Mediterranean; and, backed up by Roman forces ashore, they did their work so thoroughly as to put down piracy in seas over which that curse had unceasingly brooded.[3]

Meanwhile the need of policing the seaboard carried Rome further and further inland, until at last she found a scientific frontier in the deserts of Assyria, Arabia and Æthiopia; and so, in the search for security for her food supplies, the Roman Empire became in effect a Mediterranean Empire. Students of naval history will understand why that Empire

[1] See below, pp. 158–61.
[2] *Mediterranean Pilot*, v, 134.
[3] See Gibbon, *Decline and Fall* (ed. J. B. Bury), i, App. 5, for a good editorial note on Rome's naval stations.

lasted longer than other Empires of the past. Its duration was assured by fleets holding the central area of that vast dominion. Apart from these fleets, living spider-like along the lines of communication of that Empire, the organism would have been unwieldy and weak. Thanks to the navy, holding the interior lines, Rome gained (all unwittingly, as I believe, for naval strategy is a science slowly built up as the result of long experience, it does not come by instinct) the finest position conceivable for controlling the then known world. She could send expeditions easily and quickly either to Spain, Africa, Syria, or Asia Minor: also her fleet held apart those lands and prevented concerted action between malcontents in those separated areas. I will venture to assert that no country has ever possessed so splendid a position for the exercise of naval control; and herein we may find the chief reason why her sea power lasted longer than that of any great nation. The Mediterranean was the finest asset in Rome's imperial economy. Horace peevishly called that sea *dissociabilis*;[1] but it was so only to the enemies of Rome or to sea-sick Sybarites like Horace. To her soldiers and her merchants the Mediterranean was eminently *sociabilis*.

Other reasons for the durability of the Roman Empire lay in the character of their people, in the strength of their land base, and in their control of

[1] Horace, *Odes*, I, 3.

timber and metals. Let me briefly explain these three assertions:

(1) Roman character had been formed by centuries of tillage of the soil. It therefore had the steadiness and persistence of ploughmen; and in this respect the Romans far surpassed their enemies. The Phœnicians were essentially traders. They therefore thought too much of immediate gain to build up a lasting colonial system. Their posts planted oversea were little more than factories. Carthage, by far the greatest of them, was weakened by greed of money. As Montesquieu says: Carthage, with her wealth, made war in vain against Rome and her poverty, virtue and constancy—qualities which are never exhausted.[1] Indeed, it was not the government of Carthage, but Hamilcar and Hannibal who alone made her formidable. Apart from those men her actions were often spasmodic; and even her maritime policy was often downright weak, even stupid. As for the Greeks, the very nature of their land held them apart and developed brilliant but unstable individualism. In the last resort Rome's victory over these rivals was one of steadfastness over instability, of iron over quicksilver. Sea warfare, even more than land warfare, must be waged thoroughly and persistently to be effective. Ultimately the issue depends upon the grit of the people.

(2) The land base counts for very much in mari-

[1] Montesquieu, chap. 4.

time struggles. It must be big enough and rich enough in natural resources to enable a people to maintain fleets and train oarsmen for generations. Now, peoples having a small land base like the Phœnicians, the Greeks and even Carthage (for she could not count on her African subjects), cannot afford the waste of man power which long maritime wars necessarily entail. Only a small percentage of the population takes naturally to the sea; only they make good seamen, and they cannot be made in a hurry. If we turn to modern history we find that in turn Amalfi, Genoa, Venice, Portugal, and the Dutch Netherlands had only a short spell of naval supremacy. Their lead at sea demanded that they should throw all their man power, all their skill, all their wealth, into naval action; and this they could do only so long as the land powers at their rear left them unmolested.

But such freedom never lasted long. In turn Nebuchadnezzar and Alexander the Great overwhelmed Tyre and Sidon; Philip II of Macedon exhausted the Greek city States: Massinissa harassed Carthage. If we turn to the modern world we see the same general tendency; for the greater Italian States or the Emperors or the Turk squeezed the seafaring energy out of the seafaring Republics, Amalfi, Genoa and Venice. Also Philip II of Spain absorbed and weakened Portugal, and the invasions of Louis XIV drained Dutch vitality away landwards and reduced them to the second rank at sea.

These nearly parallel cases enable us to understand why Carthaginians and Greeks were overpowered by Rome. After she had conquered three-fourths of Italy she held strongly the central peninsula of the Mediterranean;[1] and her conquest of Sicily gave her a superb strategic position. She also had a large and (as the event proved) faithful population which clung to her, even after Cannæ. Such a power was certain ultimately to beat the fickle and schismatic Greeks or ever-mistrusted Carthage.

(3) Rome was also fortunate as regards the *matériel* of a fleet. In Italy alone she had forests large enough to build her fleets for age after age. Also, early in her sea career, she acquired Corsica and Sardinia, which contained plenty of good timber— not to speak of Elba, famous for its iron. Contrast this with the condition of the Greeks. They had no extensive forests of their own near the sea. Attica especially was almost bare of trees except the olive, which is nearly useless for shipbuilding. This fundamental defect shortened the supremacy of Athens at sea. She and all other Greek cities depended on the forests of Macedon, Thrace, Phrygia or part of Crete. I suspect that the reason for the falling off of other Greek navies was due largely to the exhaustion of timber supply. Carthage, also, after she lost Corsica,

[1] See Strabo, VI, 4, on the central position of Italy.

Sardinia and the Balearic Isles, must have had difficulties in finding enough wood to build great fleets; for there is little large timber on the coasts of North Africa. Perhaps this accounts for the weakness of her maritime policy at certain crises, which otherwise is inexplicable.

Contrast with her precarious position the advantages possessed by Rome. When mistress of Italy, she had plenty of forests near to the sea; and, as she extended her dominion, all the other timber-producing lands of the Mediterranean fell to her. No wonder that her sea power outlasted that of her early rivals. Indeed, no State has ever possessed such a monopoly of naval *matériel*; and, perhaps for this reason, no power, not even England, has possessed maritime supremacy during so great a space of time.

In fine, the naval supremacy of Rome both in the West and East Mediterranean girdled her with two impregnable shields. Neither Africa nor Spain, nor the rich lands of the East could attack her; while owing to her dominating central position and to her fleets she could, and did, control them. When the danger finally came, it came, not from the west, or south, or east: it came from the forests of the north.

CHAPTER VI

THE MEDITERRANEAN EMPIRE
AND ITS INFLUENCE

In the ancient world the growth of a State to vast dimensions led to monarchy; and, as the expansion of Rome oversea was followed by long years of civil strife, the monarchical trend became very marked. Pressure from the sea made it irresistible. For, the worse the disorders in Italy, the more she depended on foreign corn, and the less were her factions able to keep up an efficient navy and thereby assure the transport to Ostia or Puteoli.

The resulting food crisis came to a head during the civil war which followed on the death of Julius Cæsar. In that year of utter confusion, 44 B.C., when his great-nephew, Cæsar Octavianus, Antonius and the party of Brutus were at open feud, Sextus Pompeius gained command of a fleet. All the discontented and desperate flocked to him; and he soon swept the sea so completely as to cut off the corn ships on which depended the chief food supply of Rome and other Italian towns. Shakespeare thus picturesquely summed up the situation:

> No vessel can peep forth but 'tis as soon
> Taken as seen; for Pompey's name strikes more
> Than could his war resisted.[1]

The son of the man who had crushed the pirates now

[1] *Ant. and Cleop.* I, sc. 4.

seemed about to starve out Rome and starve it from the sea. But his effort failed, perhaps because he lacked the force of character necessary for success. Octavianus found means to collect ships and to bribe Menas, one of his captains; and in 36 B.C. the skilful handling of the Roman fleet by Agrippa off Naulochus in the Lipari Islands put an end alike to the career of Sextus Pompeius and the danger of starvation for Rome.

Again in the Battle of Actium (31 B.C.) the skill of Agrippa in handling the light Liburnian galleys, called *lembi*,[1] first puzzled and then dismayed the crews of Antony and Cleopatra; but their discontent at Antony acting as her general probably explains the many desertions and final rout.[2] Thus, again, the future of Rome was decided at sea; for Actium ended all danger of the Roman Empire breaking into two halves. Besides, it assured to Octavianus (soon to be styled Cæsar Augustus) the complete control of Egypt and therefore of a vast supply of corn. Never, indeed, have maritime affairs affected the form of government of a State more decisively than the campaigns which culminated at Naulochus and Actium; for the distress at Rome, when its corn supplies were cut off, told potently in favour of a dictatorship to save the State. It is significant that,

---

[1] See Torr, *Ancient Ships*, pp. 16, 115, 116. They now tended to replace the heavier and slower warships.

[2] See W. W. Tarn in *J. H. S.* xxi, pp. 173 ff.

after the victory of Naulochus, the city erected to Cæsar Augustus a golden statue bearing the device "To Cæsar, the restorer of peace by sea and land".

In fact, though the Roman Empire has generally been deemed the outcome of military prowess, it is clear that naval prowess, so essential for guarding the city's food supply, even more directly contributed to the perpetual dictatorship; for Augustus and his successors possessed command over the corn supplies of Africa and Egypt, and by them could pamper the populace with the *annona*, the yearly tribute of corn.[2]

Roman historians for the most part laid little stress on the naval factor as tilting the balance in favour of the Empire. But naval affairs were, as they still are, shrouded by a veil of mystery to all landsmen, while military affairs blare forth a presumptuous priority. In the ancient, as in the modern world, the navy is the silent service. It does not trumpet its services.

Moreover, the Romans were a land-loving folk. Therefore they rarely noticed, and their writers still more rarely recorded, doings on the sea. The truth is, they disliked that element. Though they had to do with the most glorious sea in the world, yet they never indited a poem to it. Their attitude towards

[1] See Tacitus, *Annals*, i, 2: also, later disturbances at Rome owing to high price of wheat (*ibid.* vi, 13; xii, 43). Note too the dash of Vespasian from Judæa into Egypt to capture the corn fleet, which decided his succession to the principate.

even that usually placid expanse was one almost of dread.[1]

On the whole, Roman literature contains few descriptions of sea-borne commerce. The Romans were not a commercial people. They despised trade, and left it to Greeks and other easterners. Accordingly, ancient historians considered it beneath their dignity to treat Economic History,[2] and in this respect their work is a somewhat superficial survey of life. For instance, Strabo, that eminent geographer, who flourished about 30 B.C., travelled widely, and described the ports which he visited, especially Gades, Massilia, Corinth and Alexandria, at the last of which he long resided. He noted their streets, their fine buildings, their markets, temples, etc., but clearly took less interest in the harbours, ships and the ways of seamen and merchants. He recorded, however, the fact that over 100 vessels were engaged in the trade with India.[3]

Let us now glance at some of the wider results of Roman maritime supremacy. A new and striking characteristic of the Mediterranean lands under the early Roman Emperors is the predominance now acquired by the land-masses bordering that sea. Whereas in early times small cities like Cnossus,

[1] See note at the end.
[2] See Charlesworth, M. P., *Trade Routes and Commerce of the Roman Empire*, p. xiv.
[3] Strabo, II, 5, 12.

Tyre, Sidon and Athens led the world, now the rise of the Empires of Alexander the Great and of Rome has altered all that. The city States have gone and world supremacy is vested in the Roman Empire, whose colossal bulk is undergirded by a universal sea power.

The change from the monkey-like feuds of Greek cities and the mushroom growth of the later oriental monarchies to the Mediterranean Empire of Rome ministered incalculably to the peace, order and material comfort of mankind. After her suppression of piracy, commerce leaped ahead, and civilization rose from the cottage or caravanserai stage to that—shall we say?—of a Hadrian's Palace, spacious and colossal, in which the great inland sea was the *atrium* and the provinces were the chambers. Yet even Roman persistence could not have made, much less maintained, this world fabric but for the binding power of a great navy and varied sea commerce that knit together and enriched the provinces. What wonder that two of them, Pergamum and Bithynia inaugurated the worship of Augustus and Rome?[1]

Thy shores are empires, changed in all save thee

—so sang Byron as he apostrophized the "inland ocean".[2] But the share which that sea had in furthering Roman rule and civilization has, I believe,

[1] Ferrero, v, 12.
[2] *Childe Harold*, canto IV, stanza 182.

never been duly emphasized.[1] The Roman Empire survived the strain of the removal of the capital from Rome to Constantinople in or about A.D. 330, but chiefly because from the new capital, as from the old, that imperial people continued to control the Mediterranean.[2]

Viewing the influence of sea power more widely, we may infer that it tends to assimilate the coast-dwelling peoples concerned. For it fosters an extensive commerce; and such commerce ultimately draws together races previously strangers and wholly diverse in customs. Great stores of food, clothing and ornaments, when poured in for decade after decade, inevitably replace the local products by those which are cheaper, or more showy or useful. Consequently, life becomes more standardized, to use a

[1] E.g., neither by Gibbon, Montesquieu nor Ferrero. Gibbon in his excellent account of the Empire in the Age of the Antonines (chaps. I–III) fully describes the army, but very briefly dismisses the navy. He computes the total force of both at 450,000 men. But is it not clear that this small force could not have controlled and protected so vast an Empire but for the multiplying power of an invincible navy which held the interior and therefore shorter lines of the Mediterranean? Possible enemies were spread out on a vast oval circumference and could not act in concert. This strategic fact (not noticed, I believe, by any Roman historian) goes far to explain the seemingly miraculous control of Rome over Mediterranean peoples.

[2] See Diehl, C., *Byzance*, pp. 51, 52, for a very brief notice of her sea power.

modern expression. We see that process going on rapidly all over the modern world; and it went on in the Mediterranean world. Rome and Italy in general set the fashion for the Mediterranean peoples, though the East also began to orientalize Rome. Thus, the smaller units suffered a loss of individuality as they became more or less fused in the vast melting-pot of the Roman Empire.

In truth, the grouping of mankind in great masses was not altogether a gain. The more advanced peoples, like the Greeks, lost their individual charm and their prosperity as Rome's fleets poured in her legions, laws, customs and products;[1] and in the train of the *Pax Romana* came a somewhat numbing monotony.[2] Gone were the days when Athens and Sparta could fully develop their own life in marked individualism. Greek culture was somewhat over-shadowed by the showy, vulgar cosmopolitanism of Romanized Corinth. In Greece, as elsewhere, famous city States now figured at best as municipal units, more or less free, in great Roman provinces.[3]

We can here consider only one example (and that probably the worst) of the Romanizing and materializing of ancient States, viz. Egypt. That land, long in a state of decline and weakness, fell to Rome as one of the results of the Battle of Actium.

[1] Charlesworth, pp. 126–8.
[2] Ferrero, v̇, 3, 337.
[3] Reid, J. S., *The Municipalities of the Roman Empire.*

Or rather it fell to the victor, Cæsar Augustus; for he and his successors kept Egypt as a personal possession. *Domi retinere* is the phrase of Tacitus in this connection,[1] i.e. the Emperor alone appointed the administrators of Egypt, and did not share that prerogative with the Senate, as was the case (nominally at least) elsewhere. Indeed, he took over the absolutism of the Ptolemies and owned the land in Egypt.[2] Herein we find one of the chief bases of the imperial authority. That authority originated very largely in the control of the food supply of Rome, and it remained the corner stone of the imperial edifice. The Emperors extracted all the corn they could out of Egypt and fed the Roman populace with it.

Of how much was Egypt deprived, and by how much was Rome bribed? Mommsen reckons the amount at no less than 20,000,000 Roman bushels a year from Egypt, which was one-third of the whole; and the total was even greater when the capital of the Empire was transferred from Rome to Constantinople.[3] Needless to say, the extraction of this mass of corn from Egypt led to much discontent; and risings were frequent, not only among the fellahin

[1] Tacitus, *Histories*, i, 11.

[2] Rostowzew, *Studien zur Gesch. des Röm. Colonat.*, quoted by Heitland, *Agricola*, p. 204. See too Vogt, Dr J., "Römische Politik in Ägypten", in *Der alte Orient*, 1924.

[3] Mommsen, *Provinces of the Roman Empire*, ii, 239.

(crushed then as ever before) but even in the half-autonomous city of Alexandria, which benefited by the shipping of those vast supplies. Indeed, the corn trade and other transit trades of the produce of India, Arabia and Æthiopia were so immense as to raise Alexandria to the position of second city of the Empire, almost rivalling Rome herself in size and wealth. But this mushroom growth overshadowed the old Egyptian culture (long wilting), which now practically vanished. It is sad to read of the Egyptians as wholesale manufacturers and exporters of linen, glass and paper. In their case, then, as in that of the Greeks, art and literature suffered by the douche of western influence. The new sea contacts, which levelled up the backward peoples of the Mediterranean, especially those of Gaul and "Africa", levelled down the ancient leaders of mankind.

We know comparatively little about this commercialized Egypt, which contained some 8,000,000 souls;[1] for the destruction of the great library of Alexandria by the Saracens swept away the chief sources of information. But it seems likely that the change to wholesale commerce was vulgarizing. In Egypt life tended to become prosperous but mechanical.

It is impossible here to examine the economic results produced by the immense quantity of corn poured into Italy from Egypt. But the free, or almost

[1] Mommsen, ii, 258; Charlesworth, chap. ii.

free, distribution of corn by the Emperors seems to have completed the ruin of Italian farmers and the demoralization of the dole-fed populace of Rome. In these respects the oversea corn trade of Rome, or rather its abuse, proved to be a leading cause of her final decline. A fundamentally agricultural people cannot but deteriorate when it gives up the attempt to till its own land and drifts to a huge pleasure-loving capital, there to be spoon-fed from abroad.

The commerce between Alexandria and Italy was fed largely by the greatly increased trade with India. There seem to be good grounds for believing that the advantages obtainable from the regular monsoon winds of the Indian Ocean did not become known to Roman traders until after the Augustan Age.[1] Thenceforth, trade with the East Indies increased rapidly, the favourite route being direct from Puteoli to Alexandria, thence up the lower Nile to a point near the Red Sea, and by it direct to India. This route, apparently, absorbed much of the eastern caravan trade to the Syrian ports, and of that through Persia to Trapezus; for the land journey was both slower and less safe so soon as Augustus cleared the pirates from the Red Sea.[2] The designed concentration of several trade routes on the lower Nile and Alexandria also led to a great increase in her commerce and

[1] Warmington, E. H., *Commerce of the Roman Empire with India*, pp. 5, 10, 43, 96.

[2] Strabo, II, 5; Warmington, pp. 16, 38, 102.

therefore in the size of the ships plying between that port and Puteoli—a topic to which we shall return presently.

Perhaps it is not too fanciful to suggest that the growth of Alexandria, its wholesale traders and its shipping, presents a counterpart to that of New York with its vast exports of corn in fast freighters, which have drained trade away from smaller ports. Substitute for the Mediterranean the Oceans; for the Alexandrian corn ships these modern freighters, and you will observe some curious analogies between the post-Augustan commerce and that of the twentieth century. There is a similar tendency to mass production, mass concentration at one or two favoured focal points, and export in vast bulk along the safest and quickest routes; also a decline of less-favoured lands, of smaller ports and of smaller ships.

On the other hand the Roman Empire had one great advantage over the modern world in that it nearly always possessed internal free trade. From Gades to Alexandria and the Red Sea there were, in general, none of the customs barriers which have arisen in the last sixty years, burdened as they have been with a narrow and jealous nationalism. That curse was absent from the Roman Empire, which encouraged free exchange. Thus, except at short intervals, free trade held good over a larger area than has ever been known since. Also Roman citizens were free to pass through all its parts. We never read of Pliny the younger requiring a passport for his journey to Bithynia, or St Paul either when he planned to go to Spain. Seeing that the Romans bestowed on the Mediterranean world the boon of free intercourse, we moderns should refrain from boasting too much about our superiority over them in speed of travel. Steam power and speed are immense benefits; but, curiously enough, they have, since 1870, been impaired by the increasing spread of customs barriers; and (strange paradox) the greater the triumphs of transit, the greater have become the political obstacles to their due utilization. If Pliny or St Paul could revisit the scenes of their former travels, would they marvel more at the power of modern machinery, or at the stupidity which pens up all the Mediterranean peoples in separate cages? Certain it is that, while we have almost annihilated space, we have, for the present, lost the "freely sell, freely buy" spirit which the slow-moving Romans very effectively practised. I suggest that some of our economists might do well to examine how far the long and continuous growth of prosperity in the Roman Empire was due to unimpeded intercourse over that vast and varied area; also, whether the quick alternations of booms and slumps in our far larger world are not the result of rapid exploitation, swift marketing and artificially impeded intercourse.

To recur to a few of the leading facts in the vast

trade of Rome with the East Indies, we may note that her great sailing ships needed less than 20 days to accomplish the voyage from Puteoli to Alexandria during the season of the Etesian winds of the Ægean and eastern area (July-August), though the return voyage might have to be made at first due north to Myra in Lycia if westerly winds prevailed; and off Rhodes the Etesian winds generally compelled a turn southwards under the lee of Crete, as indeed happened to St Paul's ship. Altogether the return voyage was a tedious affair, often taking 70 days or more if the winds were contrary. On the other hand the journey up the Nile and down the Red Sea was generally helped by those northerly winds; and, if the monsoons of the Indian Ocean were used to the full the journey from Rome to India and back might, according to Pliny, be accomplished in a year.[1]

Of course the growth of Roman trade with the East Indies was not all to the good. Though the horizon of the simple old Roman life was immensely widened when the Mediterranean became largely a corridor to the Indian Ocean, yet the inflow of oriental luxuries worked harm both morally and materially. The use of gems, silks, unguents and ivory became so lavish that some of the Emperors sought to impose sumptuary laws; but the Roman matrons succeeded in driving their chariots (so to speak) through the imperial edicts; and the sense-

[1] Warmington, pp. 48–51; Charlesworth, pp. 23, 62–4.

less waste continued until Italy lost far too much of her wealth; for her exports of wine, glass, coral, flaxen, woollen and metal goods, and even slaves, were far outdone in value by the luxuries imported from the East. In fact the great freighters from Alexandria to Puteoli often returned more than half empty or even in ballast.[1]

The new contacts with the East were also so alluring that Juvenal complained that all the vices of the Syrian Orontes flowed in up the Tiber;[2] but, though several of the imported cults were grossly immoral, yet the creed of Mithras, god of light, was elevating; and the general result of the jostle of new beliefs was the decay of the old Roman paganism and the prevalence of moral apathy or despair which left the field open for the lofty doctrines of the Stoics or for Christianity.[3]

The rapid spread of Christianity over the Mediterranean world was undoubtedly furthered by the suppression of piracy—an exploit more wonderful for the sea-hating Romans than their conquest of the land—and the resulting growth of fleets of really great merchantmen. To the latter development we must now turn our attention.

[1] Charlesworth, p. 7; Warmington, pp. 15, 26, 163, 270–4, 318; Frank, T., *Economic Hist. of Rome*, pp. 251–3.

[2] Juvenal, iii, 63.

[3] Glover, T. R., *Conflict of Religions in the early Roman Empire*, chaps. 1, 2.

No satisfactory account has survived of the construction, size, rig and seaworthiness of the great corn ships which plied between Alexandria and Italy. Perhaps the details were trade secrets, or else they were deemed below the dignity of history or even the notice of letter-writers. But we know from the representation of one of them on a Sidonian sarcophagus, probably of the second century A.D. (see Frontispiece), that they were far too large for oars (though two huge paddles at the stern still served as rudders); that they carried a huge mainmast fitted with one square sail and perhaps also a triangular topsail; also at the bow a much smaller mast or bowsprit fitted with a small square sail (ἀρτέμων).[1] Clearly the latter was used to keep the ship well before the wind in a gale; and this was the use to which it was put during St Paul's shipwreck at Malta.

It is worthy of note that three out of the four long journeys of St Paul were almost entirely by sea; and, apparently, he was never in peril from pirates, though he often was from robbers on land. But he suffered three shipwrecks, in one of which he was "a day and a night in the deep".[2] Nevertheless, he made his plans for voyages (of course in the sailing season) with full confidence. Thus, in A.D. 56 when writing at Corinth to the Romans, he tells them of

[1] Torr, p. 89. From the ἀρτέμων (i.e. hanger) the sprit-sail has been evolved. See Contenau, *La Civilisation phénicienne*, p. 272. [2] 2 Corinthians xi, 25.

his plan to visit Rome and then proceed to Spain.[1]
Think of it! A Jew of Tarsus plans from Corinth a
journey to Spain, *via* Rome. Is not that one of the
marvels of the ancient world?

St Luke's account of the last voyage and fourth
shipwreck of St Paul is the most vivid account of a
voyage and shipwreck in the whole of Greek and
Latin literature. Let us therefore examine it in some
detail. He was then going as a prisoner on board
ship from Judæa towards Rome, under the charge of
"a centurion of the Augustan band". This officer was
probably of high rank in the distinguished corps of
officer-couriers in the personal service of the
Emperor. Note that he, not the captain of the ship,
presided at the council held off Crete. In all the
apostle was in three ships; for from Cæsarea they
voyaged in a small coaster to Sidon, thence to the
east of Cyprus and along the coast of Cilicia to Myra,
an important port of Lycia. There the centurion
found one of the Alexandrian grain ships, which had
touched there, as such ships usually did during the
westerly winds frequent in summer.[2] She carried
276 persons, besides a large cargo.[3] From the

[1] Romans xv, 24. For the legend that St Paul did visit
Spain see Bouchier, *Spain under the Roman Empire*, chap. 11.

[2] Ramsay, W., *St Paul the Traveller*, pp. 315, 319.

[3] Acts xxvii. The captains (*navicularii*) were closely
watched to see that they kept time. See Dill, S., *Roman Society
in the last Century of the Western Empire*, pp. 192–5. The final
collapse was partly due to their slackness or fraud.

narrative in the Acts we see that she had at least two masts; for it was by her foresail (ἀρτέμων) that she worked into the bay at Malta. She also carried more than four anchors; for when off Malta they "cast out four anchors from the stern and wished for the day"; and yet there were other anchors that might have been cast out from the bow. Also the crew had means (ὑποζώματα) for undergirding the ship in case of a storm, so as to prevent the opening of her seams. Clearly, then, the ship was large; for it seems impossible to carry a large cargo and 276 persons on a voyage which might last several weeks, in a ship of less than 400 tons. This ship was also well equipped. Nevertheless, in face of the westerly winds she crept slowly along the coast of Lycia past Rhodes as far as Cnidos. Then she had to turn south towards Crete—evidently because the Etesian winds from the north-north-west there caught her and compelled a southerly turn under the lee of Crete.[1] There she proved to be utterly helpless in a storm, which swooped down upon them off the south of Crete. The ship "could not face the wind": "they strake sail and so were driven".

Now, all this trouble happened because this imperial grain ship had been impeded by contrary

[1] Ramsay, p. 320, gives the dates Sept. 1–25 for the slow voyage from Myra to Cnidos and thence to Fair Havens in Crete.

winds until the storms of early autumn were upon them and only then did the captain try to select a good port of Crete to winter in.[1] Then, when caught by Euroclydon (east-north-east), they had to let the ship drift before the wind during 14 days. As the sun and the stars were invisible all this time, the captain knew not where he was; he might be in Hadria (the sea between Greece and Italy), or he might be nearing the dreaded Syrtis on the coast of Libya. This passage shows vividly the danger of ships in cloudy weather. The compass not having been invented, they merely groped their way, or drifted helplessly in a gale.

There seemed to be no hope for St Paul's ship; for she "laboured exceedingly", though the crew and passengers (doubtless the two apostles included) lightened her by throwing cargo and tackle overboard. But finally the miraculous happened, and, though the ship and cargo were lost, yet all the 276 souls on board escaped ashore in the cove at Malta known as St Paul's Bay. Then, after three months' stay in Malta, St Paul went on board another Alexandrian ship bound for Puteoli. The captain of this ship had been more prudent and had kept her the whole winter in Malta. In her St Paul reached Puteoli, the passenger port used by the great grain

[1] See Smith, James, *The Shipwreck of St Paul*, chs. 1–4. The time was well after the autumnal equinox. The fast named in Acts xxvii, 9, was on Oct. 5.

ships, whether of Alexandria or of Africa, though cargo was usually landed at Ostia.

Before we notice the defects of this great freighter, let us glance at the only other surviving account of an Alexandrian corn ship. It is merely an impressionist account which occurs in the *Dialogues* of Lucian, who wrote about 120 years later than the shipwreck we have considered. That amusing satirist, who drifted about the world from his native Syria as far west as Massilia, finally settled at Athens and has left a lively sketch of a visit which he and three friends paid to the Piræus. They had heard that one of the great grain ships had been driven out of her course to the Piræus; and there they find her, seemingly at anchor, for they go on board and talk with the captain and the ship's carpenter. They then describe the ship: "We stood long (said one of them) staring about by the mainmast, to count the number of hides of which the sails were composed, and admiring that sailor, how he climbed up the shrouds, and in perfect security ran to and fro along the yards aloft, clinging fast to the tackling on both sides of the mast". Then another of them chimes in: "What an astonishing ship it is: 120 ells in length, as the carpenter told us: more than 30 ells in breadth; and from the deck to the bottom of the hold, where the pump stands, 29 ells. And what a wonderful mast! What a mighty yard it carries, and what ropes support it"! They then note its sign, the golden goose over the stern,[1] its decorations, anchors, capstans and windlasses; also the cabins, the veritable army of sailors; and, for cargo, enough corn to feed Attica for a whole year. But the supreme wonder is—that a little old man can steer this mighty mass with a slender pole fixed in the rudders.[2]

Lucian's picture is clearly overdrawn, and he may not have recorded the ship's measurements correctly. But I do not despise him as a witness, for he had voyaged about the Mediterranean as far as Massilia. Also, he was writing to amuse the Greeks, and would be careful not to make any bad mistakes to that nautical people. So I accept his lively account as of some value. But the point to note is that the rig of

[1] The sign of the corn ship. As the geese of the Capitol had saved early Rome, was not this sign a fit emblem of the corn ships on which Rome now depended?

[2] Smith, James (*The Shipwreck of St Paul*, p. 150) reckons Lucian's ship at over 1100 tons. This seems a great exaggeration. Laird Clowes, G. S. *Sailing Ships: their History and Development* (1930), part I, p. 35, puts the length of the ordinary grain ships at 95 ft., and tonnage at 250; but I cannot see how 276 people and a big cargo could be got on to St Paul's ship if she was less than 400 tons, at least for a long voyage against the prevalent winds, for $1\frac{1}{2}$ tons per head is a narrow estimate for a long voyage in which large supplies of food and drink would be needed. Also a cargo of grain needs many partitions if it is not to shift on one side when the wind is abeam. Therefore 400 tons is probably the minimum for his ship.

this ship resembles that of St Paul; also that it had
had a narrow escape. When seven days out from
Alexandria and in sight of Cape Acamas (north-west
of Cyprus) they were driven right out of their course
back to Sidon by a contrary gale: then, struggling
back to Cyprus, they were nearly wrecked in the
channel off Cilicia, and, after tacking against the
Etesian winds, finally reached the Piræus on the
seventieth day of the voyage, when, with a good
course, they should have reached Italy.

Thus, a contrary gale drives them very many miles
out of their course and towards a lee shore. Finally,
they work their way back to the strait between
Cyprus and Asia Minor. Then, after an escape from
the rocks, they get to the open and tack against the
Etesian winds (north-north-west) and so finally reach
the Piræus, probably for water. But observe that they
cannot face a gale any more than St Paul's ship could.
They too have to run before the gale. They can tack
only against the Etesian winds, which are generally
moderate. Now, it is a very different thing to tack
against a moderate wind, and to beat to windward
against a really high wind. Lucian's narrative therefore corroborates St Luke's narrative in a highly
interesting way; for it proves that these great craft
could not face a contrary gale.

Now, what was the cause of their helplessness? It
was due, I believe, to the weakness of masts and
rigging, relative to the size of these ships, which

may have been from 250 to about 450 tons. The mainmast and the mainsail had to be huge to get any way on so large a hull, even with a following wind. Further, the mainsail, at which Lucian and his friends gaped with astonishment, was made of oxhides patched together, which must have made it exceedingly heavy. How support it in a high wind? To do so in a following wind was easy enough. But the crux came in a high side wind. Then the strain on the shrouds supporting that heavy mast and sail must have been greater than any big Alexandrian freighter could well endure.

Contrast the masts and rigging of a modern barque of 400 tons. She has three masts of moderate size. She trusts, not to one enormous square sail, but to ten or twelve square sails and several fore-and-aft sails well suited for tacking. The sails can be reefed if the wind gets up. Also the ropes between the masts support them; and the strong and ample shrouds of a modern barque are equal to the strain of beating to windward against a gale; besides, the three masts distribute the windstrain to different parts of the hull. But how defective was the rig of ancient corn-freighters! It is unlikely that the shrouds of their single great mast were so strongly woven as to withstand the terrific strain of a gale of wind full on the beam. Such a wind tests the shrouds severely; and, if they broke, the mast would go overboard. Further, the strain on the timbers of a ship from a single great mast carrying a heavy sail must have been very great and would tend to open the seams.

I therefore conclude that the timber work and calking of ancient cargo-ships were too defective, and the cordage was too weak, to enable them to sail "close hauled" in a high wind without opening their seams or losing their masts. Indeed, their ships were built for the Mediterranean summer and were not expected to encounter heavy gales, least of all contrary gales or even stiff side winds. Such a feat demands stout masts, stout and abundant cordage and a mainly fore-and-aft rig on two or three masts. But this rig the ancients never evolved. And that was why in a storm an Alexandrian grain ship had perforce to scud before the wind, and trust to chance not to drive on a lee shore.

The result of our brief inquiry is as follows. The Romans and Levantines in their eagerness to get great cargoes of corn and of other eastern produce to Rome had ended by building ships whose bulk was out of all proportion to their means of propulsion or their sailing capacity. As has now been shown, their very size was a danger in case of a contrary gale; for oars cannot propel a big ship against a wind. Here, doubtless, was one of the reasons why, after two or three centuries, the great corn ships vanished, even from the Mediterranean. Thereafter, during some 1200 years, mankind went back to the smaller ships as being safer in a contrary wind. Then at the end of those 1200 years of experiment and frequent failures, the problem of beating up against a high wind was solved by the adoption of fore-and-aft sails; and then at last the Atlantic could be crossed; for by that time seamen evolved the ocean-going ship, albeit no larger than Columbus's vessel.

Even in this brief survey we have, I hope, observed enough of the shortcomings of the ships of the ancients to understand why they never crossed the Atlantic Ocean. Curiosity was not lacking, witness the myth of Atlantis, or that of the Hesperides. But their ships, which were well adapted to the Mediterranean summer, could not beat up against the prevalent high westerly winds of the Ocean. Therefore the ancient world remained essentially a Mediterranean world, pelagic not oceanic.

Nevertheless, thanks to man's dauntless efforts at navigation, that world thrice achieved an approach to unity. Even neolithic man is believed to have spread over its surface, thereby laying the foundation for "the Mediterranean race". Later, the Minoan and Phœnician seamen by their adventurous trading did much to promote the advance of civilization and comfort. They thus prepared the way for the Greeks and Romans, who did far more towards promoting a cultural and governmental unity through all Mediterranean lands. Indeed the maritime supremacy of Rome, lasting some 400 years, dwarfs, both in duration and in the lasting effects of its influence, that of any other people. Under the wings of her navy, commerce took giant steps ahead, and, working in unison with Roman law and administration, went far towards unifying those lands and forming a Mediterranean nationality.[1] On all sides the bounds of barbarism were pushed back far from the sea until Rome's Empire had as frontiers deserts or trackless mountains and forests. Her galleys assumed the offensive even on the Bay of Biscay and the North Sea; for Cæsar and his captains outwitted and routed the brave sailors and clumsy sailing craft of the Veneti near Quiberon; and, later, the admirals of the Empire devised a new and specialized navy which beat the seafaring Batavi in their own baffling inlets.[2] Also on her eastern frontier she long had on the Euphrates and Tigris a flotilla of war vessels which greatly increased the striking power of the troops watching the Parthians.[3] Thus, even at the outer circumference of Rome's Empire her navy maintained her sway; but its chief service was in undergirding the central parts of the mighty fabric, and in endowing it with a stability hitherto unknown in Mediterranean lands.

The indirect results there achieved were incal-

[1] See Barker, E., *Church, State and Study*, p. 21.

[2] Cæsar, *De Bello Gallico*, III, 13–15; Tacitus, *Annals*, II, 6, who describes the four main types of the new warships, some 1000 in all.

[3] Bouchier, E. S., *Syria as a Roman Province*, p. 35.

culably great. The priceless boon of long spells of almost unbroken peace enabled mankind to progress in the arts and sciences as never before. And in the wake of an assured and therefore progressing commerce there were formed new and generally fruitful contacts which facilitated the spread of new ideas and new beliefs. Greek literature and philosophy permeated all lands from Greece eastwards to Egypt, and westwards to Gaul and Spain. Further, it is hard to imagine the Christian faith spreading so rapidly to Rome and far beyond, if the imperial people had not promoted maritime intercourse throughout that great Empire. Viewed in this respect the Mediterranean figures as a mighty mixer of peoples and beliefs; for it connected the East with the West and promoted the interchange both of products and of ideas. It is by such interchange that mankind attains to a higher level of well-being, not only material but finally even spiritual. In truth, so vital, despite its defects, was the civilization which Rome spread over the Mediterranean world that it not only survived, but even drew fresh strength from, the barbarian invaders of the North.

NOTE ON REFERENCES TO THE SEA
IN ROMAN LITERATURE

It may be well to select for non-specialist readers some characteristic references to the sea in Roman literature; but I disclaim all attempt at completeness.

Perhaps the most picturesque expression of Roman feeling for the sea is that which is enfolded in the story of Palinurus. He is acting as the pilot of the ship of Æneas when it is nearing the coast of Italy. The sea is calm and everything promises well; but the God of Sleep assails him with the temptation to lie down and take a nap, while he, Sleep, will direct their course. Indignantly Palinurus repels the suggestion: "Do you bid me lull my senses? Am I to trust this monster (mene huic confidere monstro?)" (*Æneid*, v, 849). The calm sea, then, is a portent, a fearful thing never to be trusted. But Sleep bedews his eyes with Stygian drops and he is jerked into the sea. Æneas is left mourning that his hitherto trusty pilot will lie naked on some unknown shore:

Nudus in ignota, Palinure, jacebis arena.

That pathetic line marks Virgil's deep sense of the pathos of life and his secret horror at that terrifying and treacherous portent, the sea.

Very noteworthy, too, is the eager acclaim of Achates and his shipmates when first they see Italy low down on the horizon:[1]

......Italiam primus conclamat Achates,
Italiam læto socii clamore salutant.

[1] *Æneid*, iii, 523–4.

With their joy at the sight of Italy contrast that of the Greeks of the *Anabasis* when after endless marches they catch sight of the sea and cry "ἡ Θαλαττα".[1] That is their element. It never became so to the Romans, who, I suspect, all agreed with the smug contentment of Lucretius (II, 1, 2):

> Suave, mari magno turbantibus aequora ventis,
> E terra...spectare,

or with that hater of the Adriatic crossing, Epicurean Horace, when he even invokes the gods as prudently severing continents by the Ocean over which impious vessels must not pass.[2]

If we turn to the historians, we find that Polybius, a Greek by race, though a Roman by sympathy, says that no man of sense ever sails on the open sea for the sake merely of crossing it.[3] Yachting, then, was only the pastime of fools. And though Polybius travelled widely by sea he hardly ever alludes to his experiences. Probably they were best forgotten! And that was the general attitude of the Romans. It was that which we adopt towards nightmare.

Note also that terse phrase of Livy which hints so expressively at the misery of the new Roman legion which in 218 B.C. sailed with Publius Cornelius from Ostia to Massilia. Near there he had to go into camp in order to refresh the soldiers "not yet recovered from the tossing of the sea".[4] That time of enforced rest explains largely why the Romans failed to stop Hannibal from crossing the Rhone.

[1] Xenophon, *Anabasis*, IV, 7.
[2] Horace, *Odes*, I, 3, 11, 21–24.   [3] Polybius, III, 2.
[4] Livy, XXI, 26.

Tacitus, again, states that troops sent from Italy to Alexandria and then back after a short interval, suffered so severely that they were long weakened both in body and spirit.[1]

It is also significant that Vegetius, who wrote a treatise on the art of war, assigned four books to military affairs and only one to those of the sea. He excuses himself by stating that, as pirates and barbarians were cleared from the sea, the only fighting was on land. He then refers briefly to the two chief imperial dockyards, at Misenum and Ravenna, as amply defending the West and East Mediterranean. Thereafter he confines himself almost entirely to details as to the due season for felling timber, and states that fleets must keep in port from mid-November to mid-March, although the greed of merchants might prompt the despatch of single ships in the dangerous period of the year.[2]

As to the experiences of voyagers in a storm a hazardous case was described by Synesius, an author of repute in the fourth century of our era. He set forth in some detail the agonies of a voyage from Alexandria to Cyrene. Their ship encountered a storm from the North and finally the soldiers on board stood with their swords drawn so as to slay themselves rather than drown. At last they all struggled to land on a desert shore, which they embraced as if it had been a living mother.[3]

Nor did the ancients feel any enthusiasm about ships; and naturally so. For ships were worse than treadmills

[1] Quoted by Tucker, T. G., *Life in the Roman World of Nero and St Paul*, p. 29.

[2] Vegetius, F., *De Re militari*.

[3] Glover, T. R., *Life and Letters of the Fourth Century*, ch. 14.

for the oarsmen and often mere torture chambers for the passengers. Their progress was that of an anæmic centipede, not of a bird; and not until the toilsome creature had grown wings, could any poet burst forth into the rapturous joy of Spenser as he gazed at a pirouetting barque:

> Looking far foorth into the ocean wide
> A goodly ship with banners bravely dight,
> And flag in her top-gallant, I espide,
> Through the main sea making her merry flight.
> Fair blew the wind into her bosome right,
> And th' heavens looked lovely all the while,
> That she did seem to dance as in delight
> And at her own felicitie did smile.

INDEX